Pissed Me

Jay Gironimi

Copyright 2013 Jay Gironimi

To Bekka. I know you hear this stuff all the time, but I wrote it down for you anyway.

Table of Contents

Setting the Tone 6
"Hi, My Name is Jay and I Have Cystic Fibrosis." 10
My Origin Story 13
The Customer Service Desk of Life 17
Routine Investigation Part I: Breathing 22
Routine Investigation Part II: Eating 32
A Toddler Rides Past a Graveyard 38
The Day I Became a God 52
Cutting the Knot 59
A Utility Belt Full of Pills 70
Subtraction, Guilt and Toilet Ghosts 77
We Belong Dead 85
If Nature is so Great, How Come There's Not More of it Inside? 91
The Ol' CF Luck 97
If Nature is so Great Part II: Whale Watching 104
Terminal Illness 108
McPizza 114
Woooooo! 120
The Fun of Failure 124
Cultural Cachet 134
Law of Limitations 139
Coping 143
Solitary Refinement 152

Total Cost of Ownership 159
Stabbing the Antichrist 166
The Incredible Mucus Filled Boy 173
The Act of Creation 179
Appendix: Diabetes Food Diary 187
Acknowledgements 210
About the Author 213

Setting the Tone

Let's talk for a moment about *The Little Engine that Could.* A small locomotive engine decides to take on a job that, either because they are ill-equipped or not being paid enough, a number of larger engines have refused. The little engine takes on this job with a positive attitude, muttering "I-think-I-can, I-think-I can" all throughout and, lo and behold, he makes it! With nothing but a positive attitude, the titular engine, though horribly undersized for the task, was able to haul kilos upon kilos of high grade heroin into the valley (it's been a while since I read it). This book is obviously fiction and, if it were just being introduced today, would be the source of countless lawsuits from people who dropped a nut/ovary trying to lift things they had no business lifting. That's not to say that you can't train yourself to lift things you have no business lifting, but talking too much about that now would give away the plot of my upcoming children's book *The Little Engine that Trained, Said His Prayer, Ate His Vitamins and Eventually, After a Period of Many Years and Many Failures, Could.*

Just thinking about something is not enough to make it happen. If life worked like that, I'm sure more of us would be enjoying the gift of flight right now. The good news is, the opposite is true as well:

thinking a negative thought will not cause all of your pets to spontaneously combust. However, given enough time, something awful will happen to you. It doesn't even require much activity on your part: merely by existing, you are taking the chance that something awful is going to happen to you. I imagine, if you wait long enough, something positive could happen too, but it is a much rarer occurrence. Positive outcomes can require you to weather a number of terrible things and still be ready to work just a little more to get to where you want to be. It's not as easy as just thinking. If you've given yourself a mission briefing that goes "Okay, life is full of sunshine and rainbows!" you'll probably end up in disarray when it turns out that the road to that rainbow is covered in unicorn shit.

It absolutely enrages me when people say that all you need to do is have a positive attitude, so I have dedicated my life to proving that it is certainly possible to thrive without ever having one positive thought. Sometimes one or two accidentally get through, but the type of positive thinking that focuses on "good vibes" or "energy" is extremely distasteful to me, because it's passive and reductive. Passive in that it only requires you to hope for the best, as opposed to doing everything you can to make the best happen and reductive because it's a kind of willful ignorance (which may very well be the most pertinent problem of our time). You are ignoring all the countless twists and turns that life can take, effectively preparing yourself for only one outcome. That's awesome if everything goes according to plan, but if life has proven anything to me so far, it's this: it won't. And when the operation goes to hell, positive thinking isn't going to drag it back to safety. You need to actually do something. Unfortunately, you lost all that planning time daydreaming about your solid gold yacht.

    On the flip side, I don't want this to turn into a "pull yourself up by your own bootstraps" rant. If you've spent any amount of time in a classroom or office, I'm sure someone has told you that life is 10 percent what happens to you and 90 percent how you react to it (the original quote "Life is 10 percent what happens to me and 90 percent how I react to it" is from a writer and clergyman named Charles R. Swindoll). That would probably be a useful quote if it wasn't constantly used as a polite way to get you to shut the fuck up. When someone drops that knowledge on you, what they are probably trying to say is "Tough shakes. Get over it!"

    Teaching you to smile and eat shit for 90 percent of your life is a great way to make it easier for people to feed you shit for the other 10 percent. Do not fall for this trick. "React" is a broad word that can encompass everything from smiling and turning the other cheek to straight up slapping a motherfucker. Life is a delicate balance. I do not want to advocate violence here, but I want these two things to be very clear:

    1.) Sometimes life will hand you lemons.

    2.) It is perfectly acceptable to wipe your ass with them.

    Just be careful, because it might burn.

~~~~~

"Hi, My Name is Jay and I Have Cystic Fibrosis."

It has become less likely that my death will be a tragedy.

There was a time when the tragic nature of my death seemed guaranteed. I would die in my teens, robbed of a future by a debilitating twist of genetics; my potential squandered in a puddle of mucus.

I'm 30 now, so I've had plenty of time to squander that potential myself. Though the mucus should still kill me, it won't be quite as sad as it would have been if it took me out a few years earlier.

I was born with the genetic mutation Cystic Fibrosis or CF. Instead of gifting me with a superhuman healing factor or the ability to fire optic blasts, it makes it harder to breathe air and digest food. I can't eat and I can't breathe. It's just as useful as it sounds.

I haven't talked about it a lot. Though I show some outward signs of Cystic Fibrosis, I could just as easily be mistaken for a chain smoking derelict. I never denied that I had CF but I didn't advertise it either. For years, only my very close family and friends had any deeper knowledge of what was going on with me. Even still, I never told the whole story. It didn't seem to matter.

While it pains me to admit it, CF is a huge part of my life. To effectively shut that part of my life down to visitors and passer-by was to, intentionally or not, isolate myself from the rest of the world. In theory, this seemed like a great idea. In practice, the results have varied.

It's not an easy thing to talk about. Not that I get choked up when I mention it, but it's hard to explain how it affects me because it is the only experience I've ever known. Anytime I compare it to something else, it's complete conjecture on my part. It would be different if I ever knew a life without CF. From where I'm standing, you're all fucking weird. Maybe you should write a book about what it's like to breathe.

I kid. There are already plenty of books about normal respiration.

Though this book certainly deals with medical issues, I am not a doctor. However, I am well versed in the act of having CF. As such, this is not a book about Cystic Fibrosis itself, but a book about my experience with Cystic Fibrosis. It's also not intended to be representative of everyone's experience with the disease; many Cystic Fibrosis patients face the disease and its obstacles with poise and grace. I tend to do it with a gratuitous amount of swearing.

There's some adult language in this book. There's also some juvenile language. We're going to talk a lot about poop and mucus, because I deal with a lot of poop and mucus. Though I've tried to arrange the following stories into some kind of natural order, they're also modular, so if you are of weaker stomach, you're probably safe to skip some of the more detailed descriptions. Just know that I am very disappointed in you.

For many of you, stories of poop and mucus are the reason you're here. Or, at the very least, you're interested in how CF affects people. To that end, I've tried to keep this book from being a list of grade schools I've attended. It is my belief that you should not have to skip through 100 pages of set up to get to the dirt.

This is not the story of my life, but the story of my life with CF. There's no cure for CF, but I and many others would really like it if there was. While I truly and sincerely hope that CF is not the most interesting part of my life, it's probably the part that is most worth discussing. So, let's discuss.

~~~~~~

My Origin Story

I don't know if it rained when I was born. I also don't know if I was born in a Gothic castle ominously overlooking a quaint European village. I'd like to believe that both things are true, but I've been told otherwise. However, someone went through the trouble of doctoring up a birth certificate that discredits one of those events, so I have at least entertain the possibility that I was born in Connecticut on a night of indiscriminate weather in 1983.

Early on in my attempt at living, I had been labeled a "failure to thrive" baby. The good news was that my parents were about to save a bundle on college; the bad news was that I was likely to be dead within nine months. You'd think I would have made the most out of the nine months I was given, but I was not a very active baby. Breathing was hard and it tuckered me out quick. Add this to the fact that food wasn't something my body was prepared to handle and you have a child that acted more like a toy than an actual baby. If someone wanted to hold me, I was okay with sleeping on their chest for a few hours or more. I was so cool with it that one Sunday, while my father loudly hoped that the Raiders would cover the point spread, all I did was sleep on his chest. It was cause for alarm, but I was still under warranty, so I was brought to the doctor's office for repairs/return.

I don't remember how this visit went, but I had imagined the doctor taking a look at me, mulling over my symptoms in his mind and trying to piece them together into a diagnosis. As my father recounts it, the doctor took off my diaper, I shit directly into his Rolex and he had a "Eureka!" moment.

Notice, I did not write "shit on his Rolex." Any baby worth its salt can shit on a Rolex. Only babies that are covered in salt can shit in a Rolex. I was eating, but not really digesting or absorbing nutrients, so I had obtained the ability to inject a fiery orange liquid directly from my tiny asshole and into the cracks and crevices of a doctor's $10,000 time piece. Unfazed, the doctor simply announced that he suspected I had Cystic Fibrosis.

Cystic Fibrosis is not one of those things that you get by licking door knobs or sharing spoons. If you don't have it now, you're never going to get it. As my understanding of it goes, when your mommy and daddy go to the Baby Depot, they each have to hand the stork 23 chromosomes. These chromosomes are sent to the processing plant, where they are paired up and become the blueprint for a baby. If by some chance both your mommy and daddy handed the stork a defective 7th chromosome, you'll come out of the factory with CF.

On that 7th chromosome, there's a little section that contains the cystic fibrosis transmembrane conductance regulator gene or CFTR. This gene regulates the transmission of sodium, chloride and water through cells and promotes thin, loose mucus. When there is a mutation of the CFTR gene, the flow of sodium, chloride and water is blocked and the mucus remains thick and sticky. Depending on which one of the many glorious mutations of the CFTR gene you end up with, your symptoms will vary. But no matter what flavor you get, this thick mucus causes a lot of problems in the lungs, because it just doesn't move. Bacteria love it, as do various particles and ne'er do wells. Mucus can also cause trouble with the pancreas, blocking the flow of digestive enzymes and leading to that fiery orange liquid that erupted from my tiny asshole and, later, my larger asshole.

Aside from ass liquid, how can you tell someone has CF? Since people with Cystic Fibrosis have a problem moving sodium and chloride through cells and glands, they end up with a high amount of sodium and chloride in their sweat. That means that not only are people with CF deliciously well-seasoned, but that analyzing the amount of salt in someone's sweat is a great way to find out if they have CF.

Human babies lack the refined artistic taste of adult members of the species, so it takes a little more than the C + C Music Factory to make them sweat. Instead of the sweet rhymes of Freedom Williams, the sweat test uses some gel and a couple of electrodes to induce a little sweat on a small patch of a baby's skin. This sweat is collected and sent off to a laboratory so they can take a look at its salt content. If your baby is salty as a sailor's language, congratulations! Your bundle of joy has Cystic Fibrosis.

My sweat test came back positive, which wasn't so exciting, but it gave my parents an idea of how to keep me alive for longer than 9 months. That was an idea that, even as a tiny baby, I could get behind. And while I remain partial to sleeping and shitting to this very day, I eventually learned other skills too. For instance, by the age of three I could open a child proof bottle of pills and I had added the words "postural" and "drainage" to my vocabulary. Is that normal? It feels normal to me, but, as you'll see, I'm a bad judge of normal.

~~~~~

The Customer Service Desk of Life

Every day is a gift. You should remember and cherish every limited moment you have on this Earth. Even at our lowest times, it's important to remember that positive thoughts can see us through the darkest of days.

Bullshit.

As I write this, the rest of my town is still cleaning up from a record setting snowfall. I am not. I just spent three days sleeping, coughing and irrigating my sinuses. I am unafraid to admit that I did not and do not feel like any of those days were gifts. If anything, they're the type of day that you get handed because you forgot to bring your own day from home. The only reason to accept any day like that as a gift is because the line for returns is unbearable. All you can do is hope that if another day arrives, you'll have the strength to do something other than lay face down in a puddle of fever sweat.

I'm feeling better now and if positive vibes had anything to do with it, they certainly weren't coming from me. I was spending most of my time trying to remember how to stand up, walk to the kitchen and force food on a stomach that wanted absolutely no part of it. I can't be sure if I spent more time shitting or wiping, but I can assure you that I was not thankful for any of those days.

Somehow this is a controversial thing to admit. Sure, a shitty day is better than no day at all, but that doesn't mean you need to celebrate. The generally accepted knowledge is that you should be thankful for your shitty days, because even your shitty days are better than someone else's fantastic days. I get that. If you earn more in interest than I make in a year, I think you should be thankful for every day you have. Money may not buy you happiness, but it can buy you a house to cry yourself to sleep in. However, even if you're super thankful for every day that you've ever lived, it doesn't make my day any better. It doesn't affect my day at all. So how come everyone thinks it does?

I have a few theories. The first and simplest of these ideas is mere superstition. People are afraid that if they are not thankful for their day, they might not get another one. This is patently ridiculous and easily disproved, for if it were true, I would have died sometime in 1984.

I also wonder if it started as a way for the socially awkward to shoehorn their problems into the conversation. Person X was talking to person Y about how bad their day was going and person Y replied "Oh, you think that's bad? You should be thankful! I was born without a name!" They saw an opening, took it, and then continued to exploit that opening until it became part of our culture. But really, no one has to be thankful for their day for you to complain about yours. Everyone can talk about how shitty their day was and then you can silently judge the other person for being a pansy. You get to complain and judge; it's the best of both worlds.

That leads to the idea that people think you should be thankful for every day because they don't want to hear about your problems. If someone tells you to be thankful, then produces an example that has nothing to do with you or them, like say starving children, they want you to shut the fuck up, but feel it would be tactless to say so. This happens both because some people complain too much and some people are just dicks. It's a vicious circle.

But when it really comes down to it, I believe that being thankful is about guilt. For almost everything you do as part of your daily routine, there are thousands of people who didn't do it. Thousands upon thousands of people did not stand up, wake up, sleep inside, eat, drink clean water, shit in a toilet, avoid being assaulted or make it to the end of the day. Your life could always be worse and it's not hard to be reminded of that. It's also not impossible to have problems but still have some really awesome days. Conversely, I'm sure there are people with millions of dollars that have shitty days as well, I just don't care to hear about them.*

You do not have to be thankful for every day you live. You will have some really shitty days and no one should make you feel guilty about that. But that is not a license to piss on everything. There will be good days and small victories. Sometimes they will be handed to you and sometimes you will fight like hell for them. Sometimes it's a little from column A and a little from column B. In any case, you should be thankful for the ones you get, because you may not see a lot of them. You may also see some days that make your bad days look glorious in comparison, but if it comes down to it, you can always be retroactively thankful. You'll find it much easier when those days are safely encased by time and memory.

In that way, bad days are like giant bears. From a distance, they start to look harmless, almost cute. "Aw, that bear isn't so bad." But think how uncomfortable you'd be if that bear was just in your living room, wrecking your shit and eating your family. Maybe you'd like to pet it and thank it for the opportunity. Go ahead, give it a shot. Adversity builds character.

*Actually, that's a complete fucking lie. I've watched the Metallica documentary *Some Kind of Monster* an embarrassing number of times and I have hundreds of viewings left in me. It's a movie about the interpersonal problems of a bunch of millionaire rock stars and I love it dearly.

~~~~~~

Routine Investigation Part I: Breathing

When you do the same thing every day, over and over again, it's easy to forget that not everyone else does it. This is especially true of things you can't remember *not* doing.

I've been doing airway clearance for so long that I often forget other people don't even know what it is. It's not hard to parse out what it's supposed to accomplish, but the technique might be alien. The term "airway clearance" has an accessible, but medical tone to it, and it feels like it could involve anything from pipe cleaners to a tiny Roomba that you swallow. Unfortunately, it involves neither. It turns out that you clean an airway much like they used to clean a rug in the 30s: by beating the shit out of it.

What I'm trying to say is that when I was younger, my parents often beat me. They beat me hard. They hung me upside down and slapped the shit out of me. And by doing that, they shook the mucus around enough that I was able to cough it out on my own. Well, we all hoped that I'd be able to cough it out. As you can imagine, this method was not an exact science.

At its very basic level, Cystic Fibrosis is a problem moving sodium and chloride through certain cells of the body. The problem with improper salt transport is that it makes for some really thick mucus; mucus that acts like a troublesome teen in front of a convenience store and refuses to move along. This mucus, much like that troublesome, loitering teen, makes a great breeding ground for bacteria and infection, so it's best to get it off of your metaphorical lawn in a swift and thorough manner. Sometimes, this requires extreme measures.

If you'd like to try it out for yourself, grab a friend or open minded stranger and have them sit down on a couch, chair or edge of a bed. Don't worry about it too much, where they sit doesn't matter. Now, with them sitting in the upright and locked position, you need to attempt a reverse, inverted straddle, with your face near the floor and your ass pointing up at them. You'll know you did it right if it looks like you two were attempting to do the human wheelbarrow around the room, but one of you is lazy and decided to sit down instead.

The next step is to get them to hit you. To do it right, the perpetrator of this violence should cup their hand and strike with medium force over the lungs. I like to be struck right below the shoulder blade, but everyone is different, so feel free to experiment and find out what works for you. After a few minutes of this, get up and try to cough something out of your lungs. Congratulations, you've just done postural drainage!

There are different positions and techniques to get the various parts of the lungs, but the basic process is the same. Along with breathing techniques and straight up coughing, hand-to-lung beatings belong in an elite group of airway clearance techniques that you can do without any other equipment (in this case, we're not counting your partner as equipment). But once you get bored of the vanilla beatings, who's to say you might not want to add some accessories to spice things up?

By the time I was 5, we had a folding padded support thing that helped put me in the positions needed to issue my mucus an eviction notice. It kind of looked like an upside down V and could be set up at different angles to maximize drainage. We also ended up with a postural drainage machine, which is just a very high powered personal massager that's been rebranded so that your insurance might pay for it. It consisted of a base joined by a thick cable to this thing that kind of looked like a brown shower head with a protective cap on it. This shower head would shake or, to use technical terminology, percuss. You put the part with the protective cap on your chest, side or back and then use the dial on the base to select the frequency at which you'd like to shake the shit out of yourself.

To do it correctly meant to shake the left and right sides of my chest, then roll over on to each side to get the parts of my rib cage 2-4 inches under the armpits. I liked to cap it off by turning over and hitting the left and right sides of my back and then, if I was feeling adventurous, I'd just hang upside down for a while and let the mucus flow. There were various positions and angles prescribed to promote optimum drainage, but I stopped paying attention to that after a while, because unlike other activities with positions, angles and drainage, this was not fun at all.

Each of the six areas listed above was meant to be shaken for about 5 minutes. I say "about" because 30 minutes is a long time to sit and shake your lungs, so that time would often be cut short. If I was extra congested, I'd be sure to invest the time needed to move that mucus around, but if it was a nice day outside, why should I waste all my time staying inside and draining myself when I could be wasting my time staying inside and playing video games?

When a rug is really dirty, you can't just beat it: you have to break out the shampoo. Lung shampoo arrived in the form of a drug called Pulmozyme. According to the manufacturer's website, "…Pulmozyme cuts apart extracellular DNA by acting like an enzyme found naturally in the body. Cutting up extracellular DNA can help thin mucus." (http://www.pulmozyme.com/resources/faq.html) While that is a perfectly fine explanation of the drug, it does a great disservice to the fact that Pulmozyme is one of the best things that ever happened to me (I'd rank it just below the first time I saw Alice Cooper and just above that time I bought a full size bust of Boris Karloff as Frankenstein's Monster). Pulmozyme is the difference between a lung that feels like it's full of Jell-O and a lung that feels like it's full of poorly prepared, runny Jell-O. That may not sound like much, but it makes a huge difference in being able to breathe.

Pulmozyme is a nebulized drug, which means it's used in conjunction with an air compressor and takes around 10 minutes to do. That is a small price to pay for silky smooth mucus, so I have rarely missed a dose. However, it still didn't make doing the postural drainage any more exciting. Thankfully, around the time that I started on Pulmozyme, I also got a Flutter. This small, grey, pipe-like device uses a combination of positive expiratory pressure and airway vibrations to assist with the clearance of mucus. Or, in other words, when you blow into the pipe, a small metal ball vibrates, which keeps your airways open while it shakes the mucus down. It's ingenious and much easier to use than the old postural drainage machine, but sometimes I got a little too into Fluttering and I accidentally Fluttered up some of my lunch. No pain, no gain, I suppose.

I used the Flutter until I was 23 years old. That's when I received a vest. While this wasn't a bad ass denim vest covered in Judas Priest and Venom patches, I still end up wearing it just about every day.

Of course, this isn't just any vest, this is The Vest. The best way I can describe The Vest is to say it's like a giant blood pressure cuff that vibrates at a set frequency (between 6hz and 20hz) and tries to play your rib cage like an accordion. The genius of The Vest lies in the fact that it's a hands free device with an automatic timer, so it is much harder to half ass than all the other airway clearance choices. If I ever get access to a time machine, 10 year old me will be thrilled to know that our technology has sufficiently advanced so that it is possible to play *Street Fighter II* and shake the mucus out of my lungs at the same time (I won't actually bring him The Vest because he hasn't earned it). It will also come in handy if I get a job in local radio and need to pretend I'm in a traffic copter or something, because it's loud as hell.

None of this airway clearance is any good if I'm not coughing. So to keep me coughing, I also nebulize salt water. The box tells me it's a medical grade 7% saline solution, but it tastes like regular old salt water to me. Taking a hit of salt water will get a hearty cough going for you, one that will last until long after you've shut off the air compressor. Lightly salting my mucus is also supposed to encourage my body to pump more water into it, which in turn decreases its viscosity, increasing the likelihood that something will come out of me while I'm hacking away. However, putting salt water in a nebulizer also salts my throat, my face and the immediate area, which would be more desirable if I did this stuff on a throne of French fries. As it stands, I don't. But while the saline treatment is certainly not my favorite thing to do, I like the part where the mucus is not in my lungs anymore.

Truthfully, I don't care for any of these treatments, but my dislike for them is outweighed by how much I hate the feeling of not doing them, so I shut up and suck my salt. On a good day, I can get away with an hour of airway clearance, not counting my exercise for the day. On a bad day, it helps to vest as much as possible. In fact, more vesting is usually a pretty good idea. We have a saying back where I come from: "If you can rest, you can vest."

That hour of airway clearance is really two 30 minute sessions separated by about 12 hours. When I first wake up (which, I'm not going to bullshit you, is around 2 pm), I start off with a nice albuterol inhaler to open up the airways, then I strap on the Vest for about 30 minutes. To save time, I like to smoke a little Pulmozyme and hit a little salt water while I'm vesting. I like to follow that up with at least 30 minutes of exercise, be it walking, running, swimming, gator wrestling or tractor pulling. It depends on how the mood strikes me.

Exercise counts as airway clearance too, because it gets me breathing hard and gets my mucus moving. However, I like to look at it as insurance. I figure the stronger I am, the better I'll feel when I get sick. I'm going to get sick; it's unavoidable. And when I do, my lung function is going to take a nose dive. If I'm already hovering around the ground level of lung function, that nose dive is going to bottom me out. If I can hang out around the top of the scale, I might be able to pull up out of that nose dive.

Think *Raiders of the Lost Ark*. Imagine that I am Indiana Jones and CF is a giant boulder bearing down on me. When I get sick, that boulder gets closer. By strengthening my chest muscles and doing the heavy breathing that moves my mucus up and out, I'm putting a little more leeway between me and the boulder. Even if does make some incredible gains on me, hopefully I will have given myself enough of a head start that I won't be crushed immediately. If I trip up, I'll still have some room to get up and fight.

Getting back to a world where I'm not a renowned archeologist, after I exercise, I go to work or do whatever the hell I was supposed to that day. When I come home, there's another 30 minutes of vest waiting. Since Pulmozyme is a once a day thing for me at this point, the only thing I nebulize in the second session is the salt water. Though I tend to skate by on the bare minimum of vesting, if I'm particularly involved in something—reading, writing or arithmetic—I'll add a few minutes to the last session.

I'm locked into that routine and it takes precedence over everything. Really, the hardest part of airway clearance is that I still have other things to do. I still have to go to work. The trash is starting to pile up. My clothes are starting to smell like a dead skunk was buried in them. Just standard, everyday problems. Vibrating on the edge of the bed gives you a lot of time to think about the things you need to do once you stop shaking. The world does not stop turning just because your chest is tight that day.

Also, the clock does not stop ticking. I hate going to bed and I hate waking up, which is a terrible combination of hates. That means that I tend to wake up as late as I possibly can while still leaving enough time to do my stuff. I've experimented with "Oh, I'll just do it later", but that consistently makes me feel like shit. I can't just roll out of bed, throw some shoes on and run out of the door without paying the price, but I'm used to it by now. It never strikes me as odd, possibly because since the restraining orders have gone through, I'm never hanging out at other people's houses (or looking through their windows) while they get ready for work.

That's obviously a joke. They'd be long gone by the time I even finished my Vest.

~~~~~

Routine Investigation Part II: Eating

I have been known to eat meals with other people. And while these are normally uneventful affairs (unless the meal was at Hometown Buffet, where eating is more of a feat of strength), I will admit that I am sometimes dismayed when other people forget to take their pills before they eat.

I'm fully aware that not everyone takes pills before they eat. And most of the time, my brain has no issue processing this. However, every once in a while, something slips in my brain and I am appalled that someone didn't take their enzymes before starting their Slamburger (if you've never had a Slamburger, it's a Denny's treat where they take a burger and add eggs and hashbrowns to it. I'm happy to say that my retention rate on this burger now hovers somewhere around 80 percent).

Along with making my lungs into scum filled wheeze bags, my body's inability to move sodium and chloride through my cells has made a wasteland of my pancreas. In short, it doesn't secrete digestive enzymes. Because of this, I need to take a handful of pancreatic enzyme capsules before I sit down to a meal. That means, depending upon the fat and carb content of the meal, I might take anywhere from 6 to 9 pills before I actually start eating.

If I had to come up with a word to describe the average fat and carb content of my meals, I would go with "high." Being that my body does little to nothing correctly and that capsules of pancreatic enzymes are not a perfect substitute for the real thing, I still don't effectively make use of all the nutritional value inherent in a bag of cheese balls. That means I have to eat a lot of calories to keep myself from looking like Christian Bale in *The Machinist*.

I like to say that taking enzymes is kind of like driving a car with a manual transmission: after a while you learn to do it by feel. However, even the best drivers occasionally grind gears. Although a lifetime of pill popping has made me good at estimating the number of enzymes needed for a bacon cheeseburger (right now, I'd probably be looking at 8 or 9), sometimes there are so many factors involved that I don't get it right. Maybe my stomach hasn't quite yet gotten over the milkshake I had earlier. Maybe there's just something in the burger that doesn't agree with me. Maybe I didn't eat it fast enough (enzymes have an effective range of about 15 minutes). If something's not right, I'll know pretty quickly, because my stomach will put out a warning signal that ranges anywhere from mild discomfort to "I'm pretty sure something is about to crawl out." Though they aren't always easy to deal with, without those sweet pancreatic enzymes, I might as well skip the middle man and smash my meal directly into the back of my underwear, because that's where it would end up.

On top of my digestion difficulties, in 2008 I was diagnosed with Cystic Fibrosis Related Diabetes. It had been mentioned to me as a near inevitability, but I had always hoped to avoid it because I love sugar and hate needles. Fortunately, though I have to check my blood sugar with a needle, I don't have to take insulin injections, because there are pills that work for me.

I take Repaglinide, commonly known in the US as Prandin, and it tells my pancreas to quit sucking and pump out some insulin. My main issue with it is that sometimes it works a little too well and I end up with more insulin than I bargained for. If I take too many or if my meal schedule gets thrown off, I end up hypoglycemic and I start to shake and sweat and trip over my words. It happens more than I'd like because I'm not always great at checking my blood sugar and sometimes it seems like my body just decides it doesn't need the pills and makes insulin all by itself. But, if it's easily fixed by enjoying a spoonful of sugar (or delicious glucose tablets), I won't complain.

Turning my daily treatments into a daily routine has not been easy; it has only become routine through years of trial and adjustment. I'm used to it now, but it's not easy to be told "Here's something new that you need to do every day for the rest of your life." This is especially true when you're young. At times, just putting pants on seems like a hassle; having a bunch of other things to do before you can leave the house can make everything feel like more effort than it's worth.

Luckily, certain parts of the routine kind of teach themselves to you. For example, if I eat a meal without taking digestive enzymes, I'll be fine for about 24 hours. Part of my brain might even start to think "Maybe I don't really need those pills." This is the same part of my brain that spends the next day thinking "Holy fuck, I have to shit *right now*!" and then telling my asshole to release the hot poop juice.

The need for Pulmozyme, the drug that thins my mucus, creeps up, as the viscosity of mucus changes from day to day anyway. Missing a day of Pulmozyme once in a while certainly makes me feel more congested, but it's not much different from one of my thicker mucus days. However, one time I had insurance problems and missed a full week of Pulmozyme. I stopped coughing up mucus and starting coughing up blood. It was unpleasant, but I looked fucking awesome. Not so awesome that I didn't immediately charge the $1900 drug to my credit card, but enough that I struck a few Gene Simmons poses as I spit mouthfuls of blood into the sink.

Coughing up blood is not uncommon among CF patients. If it becomes a recurring problem, they shove something through your groin and into your lungs to cauterize the offending blood vessel. When my doctor told me this, I stopped coughing for a week. In the six years since that episode, I think I've missed Pulmozyme twice.

The saline solution was a harder sell. The first time I took a big hit of that thick, saline mist, I coughed so hard I thought I was about to lose my eyeballs. I was aiming for 10 minutes of saline treatment; I think I successfully completed two minutes. It took days to build a tolerance, but I eventually managed. However, the only noticeable effects the saline had were making me cough more and making my mucus taste like it had swam up from under the sea. Neither one of these impressed on me as benefits at the time, so I quit the saline cold turkey.

Years later, my lung function was on a downward slope and I was convinced to give it a try again. It, along with intense exercise and extra vesting, seemed to pull me out of my downward spiral, so I've stuck with it. All it took was the threat of rapidly declining lung function.

I don't want to categorize self-improvement as an easy thing, but having a worthwhile goal can help you get more out of yourself than you normally would. Self-improvement is a worthwhile endeavor. Self-maintenance sucks, because you're just trying to keep things from getting any shittier. Growth is much more exciting than stasis, but self-improvement is kind of useless if you can't maintain it. So, it may not be glorious, but I'll take the pills, smoke the salt and shake my lungs, all in hopes that my body won't suffocate itself or accidentally shit itself the next time I cough (it's happened). Just don't expect me to be on time (unless you're paying me).

~~~~~

A Toddler Rides Past a Graveyard

My grandmother liked to tell a story about us riding past a cemetery. She says I looked out the window of my grandfather's pickup truck and calmly asked "Is that where I'm going?" I was three years old. Before she had time to whip up the type of gentle explanation you would give a three year old, I followed up my question with "Will you come with me?"

Since I did not follow up that question with "Because I am wired to blow and I will take this whole truck with me unless you point it towards the nearest Toys R Us," she laughed. At least, I assumed she laughed, I don't really remember. She very well may have cried. I've seen her cry over a bag of Doritos and a television remote, so it's not outside the realm of possibility that this would set her off. She doesn't remember much now, so I'm sure she'd just agree with however I decide to tell the story. Even in her better days, she was never the most reliable source of information, but the main parts of the story add up: my grandfather had a truck, I was once three years old and I've always thought about death.

I don't remember when the death thing started. For a brief period, I had thought it was because I watched *Ghostbusters* so much as a child, but that would mean there's an entire generation of children who were made eminently aware of their impending demise by four enterprising chaps from New York. I guess there's a chance that these morbid thoughts were the result of some bizarre mental alchemy that came from having CF *and* watching *Ghostbusters*, but I think just having CF is enough. Liking *Ghostbusters* just means you're human.

Based on the fact that everyone told me that I was going to live a long, eventful life, I was pretty sure I'd be dead by 18. When you continually hear how much better the treatments are getting for your condition, you start to suspect something's up. Or at least I did. I was not a very trusting child.

I remember a lot of talk around the fact that the average life expectancy for a Cystic Fibrosis patient was somewhere around 35 years old and "improving all the time." To an 8 year old, being 35 sounds like it's going to be full of rocket cars and hoverboards. I figured it would be impossible for me to live that long. So, I disregarded that number, focused on the word "average" and assumed I would get the short end of the stick (technically, 35 isn't the average age, it's the median age. According to the Cystic Fibrosis Foundation, in 2009 half of the current CF Patient Registry population would be expected to survive to somewhere in their mid-30s).

I never brought this idea up to anyone until well after I was proven wrong. Somewhere in my subconscious, I must have realized it was stupid. Eighteen was obviously an age that I pulled straight out of my ass, based completely on the idea that I would never be an adult and 18 was the arbitrary age at which I would be an adult. But also, I had the feeling that everyone would try and reassure me of my impressively strong life line and that's what got me into this mess in the first place. Some ideas can only be disproven by experience.

That's not to say I didn't talk about death. Talking about death makes a lot of people extremely uncomfortable, so I tried to do it as much as possible. A lot of people are not willing to entertain the idea of their own demise. I can only assume that they are all immortal.

Strangely enough, most of these immortals were willing to accept and discuss the fact that *other* people might die, but only in bus accidents. This has been a pretty popular refrain in my life:

"You can't think like that. Anyone could go at any time. You could get hit by a bus!"

This, of course, discounts the fact that most people do not have a bus that follows them around and revs its engine every time they cough.

In a lot of ways, having CF is a lot like being followed by a killer anthropomorphic bus. You can ignore it for short periods, but every once in a while it sees an opening and takes a run at you. And even if you manage to dodge it every time, just the act of having a bus idling next to you for your entire life will severely impact your ability to breathe. Being followed by a killer anthropomorphic bus also greatly increases your chances of being killed by a killer anthropomorphic bus. Sure, there are other ways to die, but that bus is the only one that feels the need to stalk you on your morning jog.

But having CF is not completely like being followed by that bus. Unless fuel prices have turned you into an incredibly gifted gas siphoner, that bus will fucking kill you. You can't fight a bus. You can fight CF. Through treatments, exercise, proper diet, singing, and hanging upside down, you can mitigate the symptoms. Yes, it will probably still kill me, but that doesn't mean I have to make it easy.

When it does kill me, I won't be around to notice; I will be dead. For years, I had no idea why everyone else wasn't as prepared for my death as I was (and still am). I had always felt that an early expiration date was just part of the package and we've all accepted it, so how about we go out for some nachos?

It's not that easy for everyone and it's something I feel kind of guilty about (I also feel like a dick for feeling guilty about robbing the world of the gift of me, but that's not the point right now). My family has no choice but to deal with it because even if I went the route of alienating them all by acting like a raging asshole 24/7, there would still be a part of them that felt a loss when my lungs exploded in a glorious panorama of mucus and blood (I'm pretty sure that's how it will end. Don't quote me on that). But to ask someone else to get on that train is different. That's a lot of baggage to bring into a relationship. How do you drag that through your dating life?

After a few unsuccessful attempts at relationships, I had decided the answer to that question was "Don't." Not "don't bring up CF", but "don't date." I followed through on that for about 4 years. During that time, I did occasionally dip a toe back into the water, but I quickly withdrew it when I saw that I was incapable of having an intimate relationship. For me, Cystic Fibrosis has always been an inward disease and kind of a selfish one. It requires me to think about myself a lot: How am I breathing?, Is it too smoky in here?, Do I need to rest?, Do I have enough pills for this?, etc.

Part of the problem is that I never learned communicate those needs in a meaningful way. If you never ask for help, you can't be shocked when you're doing everything by yourself. Of course, a lot of that was by design. I felt like CF was my burden and it was my duty to keep everyone else insulated from it. I assure you that self-righteous bullshit came from a sincere place.

There is a fine line between communicating your needs and making the scene all about you. It's a line I try very, very hard not to cross. And yes, I realize that writing a book about my disease is very close to toeing that line, but this book easily could have started with:

"My name is Jason Gironimi and I was one of the unlucky few born with a debilitating disease known as Cystic Fibrosis. It has filled my body with a thick mucus that severely impacts my breathing and cripples my digestive function with the added benefit of shortening my life span to around 35 years. Through a series of pills and a battery of airway clearance treatments, I've managed to beat the odds and live a life as normal as possible. This is the story of my struggle."

Fuck that book. That book has nothing to say. That's a book about a disease that has a person. And I assure you that every day of my life, I worry about sounding like I'm more disease than man. For years, I assumed the safest route was to never talk about CF. Or, at very least, never willingly start a conversation about it. If directly asked, I've always been happy to answer any questions and I never denied having a disease. I just didn't advertise it. Much like a vampire must be invited into your house, Cystic Fibrosis had to be invited into the conversation. Real noble, right?

No, it's selfish. If I didn't know how to talk about it, how the fuck did I expect anyone else to? Sure, the cashier at Chipotle doesn't have to hear about my lung disease, but my friends and family might be interested. Instead, I shut them out by never showing them a way in. I hate that Cystic Fibrosis is such a big part of my life. Absolutely hate it. But that does not change the fact that it *is* a big part of my life. To ignore that and shut everyone else out of that part of my life does a great disservice to everyone involved. My disease will eventually affect everyone I know anyway. I might as well break them in while I'm alive. Plus, as my buddy Andy will tell you, telling someone it might be your last birthday is a convenient way of guilting them into coming to your party.

All of this is much easier to type out after the fact. It's not like I just woke up and changed my mind. Living past 18 put me in the precarious position of having to ensure that I continued to live past 18.

As I mentioned previously, I did not take well to this task. I had a few lapses in insurance coverage and there was at least a week when I didn't have any Pulmozyme to thin out my mucus. This made the mucus very hard to move and eventually I started coughing up blood. It sucked, but a funny thing happens when you start coughing up blood: you ask for help. Had I not grown up on a steady diet of internet traded KISS bootlegs, perhaps coughing up blood would have been all I needed to get my life on track, but given the number of performances of "God of Thunder" I've seen in my life, I made the most of a bad situation by thinking that I looked pretty bad ass. As such, coughing up blood was merely an important first step towards realizing that "Live like you're dying" didn't mean what I thought it did.

Let me assure you that "Live like you're dying" did not resonate within the chambers of my cynical heart. The perpetuation of this advice seems to be based on the idea that we, as a culture, want to go skydiving. Maybe you do want to go skydiving. I do not. I absolutely refuse to pay money to be thrown out of a plane. They should pay *me* for that privilege. But whenever someone talks about "Living life to the fullest", skydiving always comes up. Why is that?

It's very possible that everyone else in the world is just waiting for their chance to jump out of a plane, but it's equally possible that there is a powerful skydiving lobby that inserts scenes of xtreme, high flying thrill junkies into all of our media and, therefore, into our collective dreams. Think about it.

"Live like you're dying" is the kind of maudlin sentiment I find extremely distasteful, right until I think that I might be able to use it to get me a Batmobile. Your life goal may very well involve falling out of plane; mine involves owning a car that's *supposed* to have flames coming out of the back, possibly to make up for all the cars I've owned that involved accidental flames coming out of accidental places. Sure, Batmobiles are expensive, but that shouldn't matter. Live like you're dying, right?

I tried. Unfortunately, none of that looks particularly great on a loan application. It also doesn't help that I look like exactly the type of person you should not give a loan to (nor, apparently, health insurance). I would have to live like I was dying within my means. Luckily, credit card applications are a largely faceless process and, before the housing crisis caused the US economy to turn into a Starburst-based barter system, they would give them to anyone. Those wouldn't buy me a Batmobile, but they would probably buy me enough replicas to make me feel like I was living the dream (plus one time my friend Walter stenciled some silver flames onto my 1989 Mercury Topaz. That helped).

That is not the attitude of a man who is ready to have a meaningful relationship with anyone, because that is not the attitude of someone who has figured out anything for themselves. Looking back on it now, the problem is obvious: I was more scared of living than I ever was of dying. Living meant so many things: jobs, bills, rent, relationships, insurance, etc. Handling all that is a precarious balance and you can see people fuck that up without having a fatal disease. How was I supposed to handle all of that and all of this mucus? I have never, ever been scared to die and that's a problem. I would have to learn. And to learn, I would have to get some skin in the game.

To do that meant I would actually have to play the game. Having a disease did not and does not absolve me of living and responsibility. If anything, it means I have to try harder at these things, not give up on them. Just jump in with 100% commitment and fuck up until I get it right.

The financial stuff was hard to deal with and most likely always will be. Having a disease is not free and finding a job that you can do *and* provides insurance is easier said than done. But financial issues are all quantitative. There's a clear goal. You know what you need. You just need to figure out how to get there.

Emotional issues are more complex and feel more dangerous. If my bank account was cleared out right now, I wouldn't be happy about it, but there are steps to take to remedy that problem. Putting a piece of yourself in someone else's hands is terrifying. It's not like you can just go on the internet and pick out another partner.

Of course, the internet is where I met my fiancée, so maybe I'm full of shit. I was very clear about all my medical baggage upfront and I even told her about some of the emotional baggage. Amazingly, she still agreed to meet me. With her living on Long Island and me in Connecticut, there was a little distance between us, so meeting for the first time took planning, but maybe the distance made it somewhat less threatening. I wasn't completely sure that she wouldn't skin me alive and make herself a custom seat cover, but she probably thought the same of me.

As of this writing, we both remain unskinned. And our relationship is fantastic, even if we still haven't solved the problem of the distance between us. We're working on it though. Change takes time, especially since I can't go begging on the street corner for medical insurance.

There's a part of me that felt like I was protecting people by not letting them get close to me, like my emotional distance would insulate them from my eventual absence. I am completely embarrassed to admit that now, because it's probably the most narcissistic thought I've ever had. In my defense, those are still not easy waters for me to navigate. The difference is that I'm no longer afraid to try.

Not too long ago, my fiancée, Bekka, asked me if I was going to get sick and suddenly die on her. Not in the way that I'd die on top of her, but in a more general sense. I didn't know what to say and, to be honest, don't remember what I said. I remember what I thought though. I thought about how it's important to let her know how much I care about her right now, because someday I'll be dead, and that makes it much harder to show emotion. I didn't think that was exactly what she needed to hear at the moment, so I kept it to myself, but it rang true for me.

It may not always be easy to express these feelings, but if you don't want your loved ones paying a cold reading con-man an exorbitant amount of money in hopes that he can talk to your spirit, you need to make your case now. I understand the trepidation; I'm not very demonstrative with my emotions, so I'm probably not going to come up to someone and say "I value our time together." That's just too on the nose for me.

Luckily, there are other ways to convey the same meaning: take a little time to tell a story, tell a joke or even try shutting your mouth and *listening* to a story. These are all things that, when done properly, convey the same meaning as "I value our time together." Think of them as emotional synonyms. If those don't work for you, find something that does: buy a friend lunch or key someone's car for them. They'll know what you mean.

If, at some point in your life, you are told you are going to die, here is the most pertinent question to ask: how do I not? Of course, the first answer will be "Well, everyone dies", because everyone's a goddamn joker, but after you get past that, if there is something you can do to stay the hand of the reaper, you need to do that. There's also a chance there's nothing you can do. Sometimes, the only thing you can do might seem worse than actually dying, but that's a decision you need to make for yourself. Either way, you are not absolved of being alive at that moment. If you can't get out of bed in the morning or you're feeling overwhelmed, that's fine. Things happen and the people that matter will understand that; you just have to tell them. No matter what anyone tells you, they do not have a telepathic link into how you're feeling. So next time you get the chance, tell them.

I have no idea what the future holds; I've proven this again and again. As I write this, I just passed my 30th birthday and I'm also engaged to a wonderful woman. Those are both things I never thought would happen. But here we are. Though I hope our 7 year age difference balances out the difference in our life expectancies, obviously I will get sick from time to time and at some point I'm going to die. Hell, either one of us might get hit by a bus. We'll deal with that as it arises. My life goal no longer involves owning a Batmobile; it's now about making sure I live long enough so that Bekka and I can turn into an old, bitter married couple. It's about telling stories, listening to stories, calling bullshit on stories. It's about being an active part of the process or throwing rocks at the process, whatever the case calls for.

Not that I'd refuse a Batmobile if one showed up.

~~~~~

The Day I Became a God

Pac-Man 2 was released in 1994, finally answering the big question we had at the end of the original *Pac-Man*: Does Pac-Man live in a house that looks like him? The answer is yes. Imagine the disappointment we all would have suffered if Pac-Man lived in an apartment.

This question was not answered via clever new twists on the maze game formula, but by dropping you in the middle of the Pac World, introducing you to its inhabitants and allowing you control over positively none of them. Rather, the game turns you into a disembodied voyeur with a sling shot, allowing you to make vague suggestions to Mr. Man, which he may or may not follow, depending on his mood. Essentially, you are Pac-Man's god.

I was probably the only person who bought that game the day it hit the shelf or, more accurately, the only child who suckered their grandmother into buying it for them. I'm not even sure why I was so excited about it. I like to think that my 11 year old mind was simply pumped up at the prospect of a Pac-Man game I wasn't terrible at. More likely, I was an easy target for effective branding.

Pac-Man 2 was the first game I played that did not put me in direct control of the main character. Even if the assholes in

Maniac Mansion got sassy from time to time, they'd still put the hamster in the microwave when I goddamn told them to. *Pac-Man 2* was different. I was in charge of this man's life, but I could not control his actions; I was more of a care taker than a move maker. This was a lot of pressure for an 11 year old.

The life he had was pretty good: a wife, some kids, the aforementioned house; but the dude had some issues with motivation. Hell, it took an act of god to get him to leave the house every day and get his baby some goddamn milk. But you can't blame the victim, as he spent 14 years of his life being controlled at every turn. When you've spent that long with someone holding your joystick at every pellet, you're bound to have problems.

Played properly, the first level of *Pac-Man 2* goes like this: when it becomes obvious that "Yes, kids really do need nourishment", Ms. Pac-Man sends Pac-Man out for some milk. To help him with this, you repeatedly jam the "LOOK!" button until he ends up at a dairy farm. Since he's spent the last 14 years living off of diminishing royalties, he didn't bring any money and he has to steal the milk. However, since an anthropomorphic ball is the least stealthy thing ever, you have to do most of the work. Luckily, the dairy farmer fell asleep guarding the one cow he owns.

However, to be super sure he doesn't wake up and have a heart attack when he sees a giant Lemonhead unlawfully milking his prize bovine, you'll need some cover. Luckily, the farmer fell asleep under a haystack. Shoot the haystack and it will fall on his head. The severe head trauma this causes will allow you to bounce past undetected.

Once Pac-Man clods his way past Old MacDonald, you'll need to draw the Man's attention to the empty glass bottle conveniently resting atop the cow's pen. Since, as previously noted, Pac-Man has some serious motivation issues, he will not just grab the bottle and milk the damn cow. Instead, you'll have to shoot a nearby crow with your slingshot, which will piss off the crow, causing him to knock the bottle off the fence and freak out Pac-Man. After Pac-Man gets his shit together, he'll see the bottle lying next to the cow and piece together the idea that he could have just milked the cow 5 minutes ago and saved us a lot of time and effort.

Sounds like a ton of thrills, right?

As it turns out, feeding children doesn't carry the same visceral thrill of outrunning ghosts. There's a reason why Kubrick's *The Shining* ends with an awesome maze chase and not with Jack Torrance going out to get Danny some milk. Our lives are already filled with mundane tasks; we do not need them in our entertainment as well.

Mundane tasks and 11 year olds don't mix well anyway, a fatal flaw in a game that seems to be predicated on the idea that 11 year olds care about hungry children in Pac-World. I imagine that somewhere there are compassionate 11 year olds, but I was not one of them. Unless Pac-Baby was going to eat some ghosts, I did not give one red fuck about his breakfast. I still don't and I probably never will.

I tried, but I failed quickly. I dutifully sent Pac-Man outside to begin his adventure and explore his world. I saw he had a dog, so I thought it would be good to have him pet his dog. Then I thought Pac-Man was enjoying that a little too much, so I shot him. Then I felt like his reaction to this was blasphemous, so I shot the dog too. Then Pac-Man got mad at me for shooting his dog, so that earned him another taste. This went on until Pac-Man threw a righteous fit, lashing out at his god for forsaking him. That tantrum left him so drained that he became despondent and withdrawn, refusing to even acknowledge my existence. He was at his lowest, wandering the proverbial beach of life and wondering why, at this lowest moment, did he only see one set of footprints?

Salvation arrived in the form of a Super Pac Pellet. Yes, his god was carrying him!

You see, unlike the normal pellets you load the slingshot with, the Super Pac Pellet is not a tool of rebuke, but a tool of reward. When fed a Super Pac Pellet, Pac-Man immediately perks up. He flies around the screen with renewed vigor, praising the light for breaking through this dark night of the soul. Though, as we all must, he eventually comes down to Earth, he does so in higher spirits. He has seen the light and it was good! Then the light shot him again for being too prideful. This process repeated itself until I finally got him stuck on a cliff, too depressed to go on.

Here was a man who brought joy to millions of people and asked for nothing but a few paltry quarters in return. I was in charge of him for 5 minutes before I tried to ruin his life.

Lest you think that I'm just some kind of monster who tortures beloved cultural icons, let's talk about the first *Pac-Man* game. I will assume that, since you are alive, you have played the original *Pac-Man*. If not, go do that now. Trust me, it's for science.

If you've already played *Pac-Man*, there's a good chance that no one told you what to do. The attract screen on the arcade version will give you a quick rundown, but most of us don't have time to sit around and watch the attract screen or have things explained to us. We're already experts, so just give us the joystick and shut up.

Starting the game will drop you, as Pac-Man, into the middle of a maze. Your job is to wander around and gather up trucker speed while avoiding ghosts. How do you know you're supposed to avoid the ghosts? Just look at them: wandering around, all different from you, those smug bastards. Keep your distance and everything's cool: you get the pills and some fruit and the ghosts get to wander around looking for their killer so their spirits can finally rest. But no matter how firmly you stand by that "live and let live" bumper sticker you placed on your car, the ghosts will eventually decide that, since you look different from them, they will chase you. You can't reason with them. Hell, you can't even come into contact with them: you'll die. They chase you for a singular reason: because you live.

If the tables were turned, you would never act like that. You're kind and noble, right? "Hey ghosts, there's plenty of room in this maze for everyone! Make yourself at home! I'm just going to eat one of these big pellets." That's when the power hits you. "Man, FUCK THESE GHOSTS!" you shout as Blinky runs crying for mercy. Mercy does not come. "I CAST THEE OUT!" you scream as you damn their tortured souls back to the Purgatory awaiting them in the middle of the maze.

The power doesn't last and you eventually come down. And when you do, you feel the regret and the remorse. You swear you'll never let it happen again. But the opportunity presents itself again and, well, fuck those ghosts.

I'm not saying that when you play *Pac-Man* you should treat the ghosts with respect and keep your distance. In fact, if you see someone doing this, you need to watch them very closely; they are not to be trusted (seriously, fuck those ghosts). And besides, it's only a game; those ghosts exist to feel your wrath, just like Pac-Man exists to feel my wrath in the sequel.

Games are not real life and I'm thankful for that. In all my time behind the slingshot, no one actually suffered, save for perhaps the grandmother who had to fork over $50 so I could pretend to shoot a yellow ball with a slingshot.

Sometimes I wonder if someone is pointing a slingshot at me. I don't think so. I don't think there's an invisible hand waiting to shoot me or reward me at every turn. But while I'm not a believer, here's the best argument I've heard for the existence of a higher power:

If *Pac-Man 2* had a "give Pac-Man Cystic Fibrosis" button, I would not have hesitated to hit it.

Cutting the Knot

I remember the time one of my mother's friends came over to sell a pair of scissors. She had jumped feet first into the dog-eat-dog world of door-to-door scissor sales and my mother did the polite thing by agreeing to an in-home demonstration. Normally, you agree to the demonstration, your friend and/or relative comes over, you express appropriate awe towards the product, say that you're very satisfied with the scissors you already own and everyone goes on their merry way. However, I was 4 at the time and I didn't get the dynamics of these situations. I just figured that if someone was coming to the house to sell us scissors, they were some pretty impressive scissors. My curiosity was piqued, so I stepped away from the television and paid close attention to the demonstration.

I could not have prepared myself for what happened next. The woman produced a penny and cut it in half. Let me repeat that so it really sinks in: She cut the penny in half. No camera trickery, no sleight of hand: the penny was torn asunder by tempered steel. Then, to demonstrate the dexterity of those powerful shears, she produced another penny and cut the rim off of it. I had never seen anything like it. I was very excited that we were about to get in on the ground floor of such an amazing technology.

Thinking back on it now, I was the only one in the room who thought we were buying those scissors. Penny cutting makes for an impressive tech demo, but our family didn't have enough money to just start cutting it in half, no matter how small the denomination. Adjusted for inflation, that penny would be worth two pennies in today's money. (This is assuming that the penny—or, for that matter, the economy—has not been abolished by the time you read this.)

I have almost no recollection of what was said during that demonstration, but I remember exactly what happened. My memory of my parent's divorce is very similar.

I remember one day my mom sat me down and said something, but I don't remember what. Whatever it was, it cut the penny of my life clean in half. I remember crying and asking for a green Fla-Vor-Ice popsicle afterward, which made me feel much better. And much like the scissor demonstration, I got to keep both halves of the penny.

I often feel like I should remember more about that moment, but I probably needed that space in my brain for Iron Maiden lyrics or something. Or maybe, given what science now knows about how memory works, I don't remember much about that moment because I never think about it. Not because it's too painful, but because I never have to.

Every day from that point on, I've dealt with the ripples of that. To this day, my mom and dad live in different houses; it's not like I can just ignore the fact that they're divorced. In fact, my brain often has trouble reconciling that they were ever together.

I dealt with a proportionally small amount of married Mommy/Daddy time; they were married for the first 5 years of my life and have been divorced for the last 25. If I didn't get used to it, it didn't matter. There was nothing I could do about it.

In the immediate fallout of the divorce, the biggest issue I had was that somehow I managed to lose half of *my* stuff, chief among these items being my original *Ghostbusters* figures and an orange plush brontosaurus. The Ecto-1 car that followed me to my next place of residence was rendered useless without anyone riding in it.

I lost most of those things because we had no place to put them. Before the divorce, my parents were renting a condo. When my mom and I moved out, my dad stayed in the condo for a while, but it was a lot for one paycheck to handle. He moved into a spare room at his friend's house, leaving a solid portion of my stuff behind and transferring the lease on the condo to my orange brontosaurus. That dinosaur may have been extremely huggable, but he just wasn't responsible.

My mother and I moved into her friend's trailer for a short period, an arrangement that limited my personal space to a small dresser with some stickers on it and required me to share a room with two other kids. For an only child used to spreading his crap everywhere, this took some adjustment.

I spent weekends over at my father's room, which was notable because the owner of the house had a CD player. For those unfamiliar, a CD player is a machine in which you place a shiny silver disc to make the music of Huey Lewis and the News come out of the speakers. I spent most of my toddler years spinning Huey Lewis vinyl on a Big Bird record player, so this was a huge deal to me. No longer would I have to count the grooves on the record to find the start of "Bad is Bad"; I just had to remember it was track 3. It was one of the first times I can remember being absolutely stunned by the beauty of this world.

My mother and I upgraded from sharing a trailer with a family of three to sharing a room at her parent's house with some pictures of Jesus. This arrangement afforded me a slight increase in personal space, but a complete decrease in the amount of TV I was watching. I'm sure a lot of you just read that and were like "good, kids shouldn't watch TV anyway," but for a child of divorce, TV is pretty much a third parent. Also, this meant that I missed the premiere of *The Simpsons*, an act for which I have never and will never forgive any of the responsible parties. They know who they are.

About a year after the divorce, my father moved into a proper apartment. The apartment complex had an indoor pool, which I was excited about. However, I was less excited that the apartment itself contained my father's girlfriend and her daughter.

As popular family lore has it, one day my father's then girlfriend and now wife, Linda, had suggested that we should have tacos for dinner and I let her and her daughter Jocelyn know that maybe they could just go to Mexico. I don't remember this but I can't deny it, because that certainly sounds like my M.O.

I cringe when I hear that story, because we're all family now, but I was 6 years old at the time and lacked the emotional tools required to process any kind of change, particularly the type that meant I had to share a parent with another child. However, it helped that this child had a Nintendo.

I had an Atari 2600 when I was younger so I was aware that games could be played on your TV, but in the years since that machine self-immolated the Super Mario

Brothers had been born. I remember the first time I walked into Jocelyn's room and saw Mario on the screen. Jocelyn and her cousins were already playing the game, so I had to pretend like it didn't just blow my goddamn mind. I played it cool, but part of me realized that the reason I didn't have my own Nintendo was because neither of my parents loved me and I was the reason for their divorce.

Okay, that's not completely true.

A lot of the reason I didn't have a Nintendo at the time was because I didn't have a space of my own. I shared a TV-less room with my mother and hooking up a Nintendo to the TV in her parent's living room just wasn't happening. Fortunately, my father's mother was a complete pushover, so I eventually just took over her living room and planted subliminal cues in my mom's head that we should move as close to Grandma Marion's house as possible. Eventually, it worked. My mother will probably tell you that us moving into the same apartment building as my grandmother had more to do with childcare than anything, but that's just because the mental manipulations worked so well.

Because our apartment was roughly the size of a small storage locker and lacked a Nintendo, I spent a lot of my time in my grandmother's living room, making a complete mess and pretending to be a plumber who jumped on turtles in a far off land. I assure you that is much less sad than it sounds.

I continued to spend the weekends over my father's house, which meant I was spending roughly 2.5 days a week adjusting to the idea of an expanded family. I probably would have ridden that process out straight into my 20s if my father didn't have another child.

I was 10 when my half-brother was born, which meant I was still young enough to not handle the idea well. I remember my father having a talk with me in his room and letting me know that Linda was pregnant. My immediate reaction was to ask how the child would be related to me and then come up with scenarios by which it could not be. Fortunately, my "What can we do about this?" phase only lasted about a week, partly because I learned to accept change and partly because, again, there was nothing I could do about it.

I was present for the birth, but not present enough to look at any of the important parts. I don't think I fully realized what I was signing up for. The prevailing attitude in the room had me figured for having a weak stomach, a notion I did little to dispel. I didn't know how to explain that, while this all seemed like a great idea in theory, I found the situation painfully awkward. I am of the opinion that there are parts of your stepmother that you shouldn't see.

I caught a solid profile of the baby coming out though, which was interesting because they had to suck him out with a plunger. It gave him a conehead for a few days, but they resisted the temptation to name the baby Beldar. Instead, they named him Jacob, which seemed like a great idea before they got him home and realized that there were now three kids in the house with "J" names. Alliteration makes it hard to remember which name you want to yell when it comes time to start yelling names.

It makes narrative sense to anoint Jake as the baby that united us as a family, but I would never want him to think he was that important (I kid because I love). Plus, that would discount the time I had a small emotional breakdown from babysitting on the weekends. I eventually got over it.

On my mother's end, she teamed up with a gentleman who really liked alcohol. This led to yelling for her and hilarity for me. He did not take too well to me, which would have been fine if we didn't live in the same house. It got kind of tense at times and much of it was my fault. I was so amused by the fact that he would get angry when I left the pizza stone on top of the stove, that I would often put it on top of the stove just for fun. If you've never heard someone use the words "pizza stone" in anger, I highly recommend it.

We ended up living in a large house out in the woods, so there was plenty of room for myself, my mother, her fiancé and his two kids, but our journey started in a tiny three bedroom apartment. This is important to note because although her fiancé's kids were only there on Thursdays and every other weekend, my mom felt we didn't have enough room in the apartment for a computer. She backed this claim up by buying not one, but two typewriters on which she made me use the typing skills I gained on my father's home computer to type out her college essays. Consider it proof that as one gets older, "Well, Dad has one!" becomes exponentially less effective.

When we moved into the house, a computer soon followed. Though it was in the family computer room and technically meant to be used by the entire family, I figured out how to record my own music on that thing and it was game over for everyone else. The computer room was right next to the living room, so sounds would often end up competing with each other. One day, while my good friend Andy and I were working on a track, there was a terrible noise in the living room. My mother's fiancée had gotten drunk and fallen asleep on the couch. While he slept he made the worst fucking noises you have ever heard in your life. This was a regular routine and I was used to it. However, Andy heard what seemed to be a team of foley artists meticulously recreating the sound of a tank slowly crushing a pile of skulls and asked:

"What's that noise?"

"Oh, that just how he snores. He does that." I answered.

"Is he watching porn?" was Andy's follow up question.

The answer was "yes." He passed out drunk on the couch, watching softcore Skinemax. Normally, you wouldn't be able to catch a detail like that over all the snoring, but we had a pretty powerful surround sound system.

It was awkward. I loved that house though. I stayed there for about 3 years and always thought about going back. Three years after I left, my mother left both the house and her fiancé behind and there was no house to go back to. She eventually married a great man who, as of this writing, has never used the words "pizza stone" in anger. We get along much, much better.

Divorce often feels like there's no one place that you belong. Not that you don't have places where you're welcome, but that you don't have roots in any one place. I know that sounds ridiculously maudlin, but it's true. Well, sometimes it's true. Other times, it felt like I had a lot of places I belonged, so it balanced out. Plus my parents generally lived within a 30 mile radius of each other, so there was never an extended period of time when I didn't see one of them.

It's tough to parse out what I learned from divorce and what I learned from Cystic Fibrosis. They feel like complimentary courses of study to me. It's an interesting thought experiment to think about how I would have turned out if I didn't have to deal with either one of them. But it's just that: a thought experiment. Both divorce and CF are indivisible from who I am. And really, I'm okay with divorce. If anything, it helped build character. One could make the argument that Cystic Fibrosis builds character as well, but I'd be willing to do without. I'm okay with divorce; Cystic Fibrosis can go fuck itself.

~~~~~

A Utility Belt Full of Pills

In 1989, the landscape was studded with bat symbols. Bat symbols every 3 feet. I was 6 in 1989 and it ruined me for life. It was the year that Batman came to the big screen.

I'm almost certain that there are a number of people who are still in straightjackets because they snapped the day Michael Keaton was cast as Batman. People went nuts. The world had enough of campy Batman. It was time that we took a man dressed as a flying rodent seriously.

I was still young enough to miss every joke in the 1966 Batman series, but I liked to pretend I knew what I was talking about (I still do). I remember talking to one of the pharmacists at the drug store my mother assistant managed and, in an effort to prove I had an opinion, I told him about how I enjoyed the Adam West Batman when I was little, but I was ready for a serious Batman. He laughed at me and, at the time, I didn't understand why. I watched those Adam West Batmans when I was 3. At 6, that was half a lifetime ago. Asshole.

Anyway, *Batman* was the first cultural phenomenon that I could actively participate in. I loved *Ghostbusters* and *Back to the Future*, but I loved them via VHS (in the case of *Ghostbusters*, it was a VHS recording of an HBO showing in which, for a brief moment, someone changed the channel right before Venkman gets slimed). *Batman* was happening right then. I didn't have to pester anyone to find me the Batman merchandise I so desired. It was right there. I'm pretty sure that if you went into any major store and knocked your cart into the shelves a few times, it would eventually fill with quality Batman products. For example, on a routine trip to the card store in the mall, I managed to talk my Grandmother into buying me the official Batman mask, pulled from the official movie mold. This was at a greeting card store! Why my grandmother ever decided to buy an $80 mask for a 6 year old, I have no idea, but I assure you that it improved my life tremendously.

Given the amount of youthful exuberance I had worked up over this, I expected to see the film on opening day. Unfortunately, back in 1989, it was pretty rare for a 6 year old to have a job or a car, so I would have to ask one of my parents to bring me. Though I usually spent weekends with my Dad, for whatever reason I was staying with my Mom at her boyfriend's house on opening weekend. I rarely outright asked my mother for things, but this was an emergency. Through some light prodding on my part, it was decided that we would all go to the movies on Saturday. This was not opening day, but I was desperate enough to accept these terms. There was some discussion of what we would see, but I paid little heed to anyone else, because asking "What should we see?" on the opening weekend of *Batman* struck me as just about the stupidest fucking question anyone ever asked.

"We're going to see *Batman*," I announced.

My mother had seen this coming, of course. She began to look at the times, which I remember being listed in a little two column ad amongst the other, lesser films.

And then her boyfriend spoke: "I don't know if he should see that. It's PG-13."

I imagine few people can remember when they learned to hate. I can pinpoint the exact moment.

Surprisingly, I showed restraint. While my first thought was "Who the fuck is this guy?", my mother would have slapped me if I said it. Instead, I went with the less inflammatory "Dad will just take me next week anyway." It worked. My leverage of broken home guilt sent us off to the movies.

Though I wouldn't admit it at the time, the shadows that flickered in front of my eyes for the next two hours were sometimes over my head. I found the symmetry of the opening robbery and the killing of Bruce Wayne's (spoiler!) parents a little confusing. I wasn't quite clear on exactly how the Joker toxin worked. I briefly thought the Joker was a robot. However, I fully understood that I had just seen the greatest thing mankind had ever created.

My dad ended up taking me to see it the next week as well. And the week after that. And the week after that. All told, I believe I saw that movie 8 times in theaters. And, as is the want of corporate America, seeing the movie 8 times was not enough for me. I demanded merchandise and, more importantly, information. I read all the comics I could get my hands on. I read interviews with everyone even remotely involved in the film. I read *Mad Magazine* for the first time. Shit, I read *Cracked* magazine. I even read the adult novelization of the film, which blew my mind by including a deleted scene of Bruce Wayne in a ski mask, riding a horse while chasing the Joker.

Did I understand everything I read? No. That horse scene briefly made me wonder if I had somehow managed to see the wrong cut of the film 8 times. That's not quite as embarrassing as the time I read the novelization of *Terminator 2* and confused "guerillas" with "gorillas," but it's close (in defense of my 8 year old self, a gorilla/machine war would be awesome). I understood even less of whatever *Mad* was talking about, but to see a bunch of adults refer to themselves as the "usual gang of idiots" while telling you that everything is pretty much bullshit was hugely affecting to me at that age. I knew something was up. It was nice to have that suspicion confirmed.

This may sound like a glorious journey of self-discovery, but let's not cut corners: I wanted to be Batman. And it wasn't just because I wanted to punch a bunch of people or because I wanted Prince to write an album about me; I wanted to be Batman because he knew everything. The Joker hijacked the TV signal and was like "I poisoned a bunch of shit, but I won't tell you what shit" and Batman was like "Fuck you, here's a list of shit you shouldn't buy." While the rest of Gotham was like "What do we do? Let's just stop buying deodorant!" Batman thought about it, realized he needed Old Spice and did what needed to be done. *I* wanted to wrestle health and beauty products from the hands of a madman.

That sounds like a crazy, narcissistic pre-adolescent power fantasy, but what if Batman couldn't breathe? What if he had a lung disease? What would he do then? I'll tell you what he would do: Batman would fucking breathe, because he's Batman. He might use some clever gadgets or he might spend a couple of nights working on the problem, mapping out the human genome and perfecting gene therapy, but he would breathe. Judging from that time I attempted to grow my own pet using nothing but an old sock and a can of Teenage Mutant Ninja Turtle Retromutagen Ooze, my genetic modification skills were somewhat substandard (looking back, I think the issue was that I was using Retromutagen Ooze. I should have asked for regular Mutagen Ooze), but I did have access to gadgets.

Batman is (usually) part of the Justice League, where he is constantly surrounded by people with incredible super powers. He has none. What he does have are a bunch of gadgets that level the playing field. Sure, Superman can fly, but Batman has a jet and a Kryptonite ring. You take the advantage where you can get it. Maybe somewhere in the back of my mind, those gadgets made me feel better about the utility belt worth of pills it took me to eat a meal or the airway clearance I had to do to level the playing field between me and the superpowered lungs possessed by everyone around me. While it's reductive to write "Batman taught me how to breathe!", I don't want to understate the importance of Batman to my development. Art, and I do not hesitate to use that word, was very important to me growing up. It allowed me to step outside of myself and my circumstances. It gave me something to strive for. You know those motivational posters that say "Shoot for the moon, because even if you miss, you'll land among the stars"? That never did dick-all for me. Instead, I shot for Batman in the hopes that I would land among normal people.

I never grew up to be Batman. It was never going to happen for me, mostly because I'm not tall enough. But I did grow up and a lot of that has to do with Batman, Spider-Man, the Hulk, Frankenstein's Monster and all the characters and stories that I've ever heard. As Picasso said, "Art is the lie that tells the truth." And while you may not agree with my definition of art, I can assure you that all these lies were very important to a child who needed a little help dealing with the truth.

Besides, if I couldn't fully grasp the novelization of a movie I'd seen 8 times, I wasn't going to learn a goddamn thing from *A Tale of Two Cities*.

~~~~~~

Subtraction, Guilt and Toilet Ghosts

Divorce presents a number of logistical difficulties. I was 5 when my parents divorced and being that "The Man" felt I was not old enough to be home alone, I required supervision. Having two single parents meant they were both working their asses off, leaving me with a number of babysitters. This was costly for my parents and frustrating for me, because I had to give my Batman speech over and over again. I imagine it was also nerve wracking for the babysitters, because although I wasn't a difficult child, I would be wary of babysitting any kid who had to take 6 giant pills before a meal. The odds of something going wrong on your watch are increased with every peanut butter and jelly sandwich. The stress probably wasn't worth $5 an hour. So, before I drove a cadre of well-intentioned teenagers to anxiety induced depression, my mother made a move.

That move was into a small apartment in Jewett City, CT. My grandmother managed the building and, since that job required her to stay home a lot, she would be able to provide the kind of quality free child care one can only sucker out of a family member. Or someone who used to be a family member. Though it didn't strike me as odd at the time, given my parents contentious divorce, it's strange to think that my mother and I lived across the hall from my father's mother. But unless my dad and my mom happened to cross paths, there wasn't any social awkwardness. And even if there was, it wasn't on my end, so I didn't care.

My grandmother gave me run of the house, which isn't too out of the ordinary, but I think it's odd that my grandfather put up with it. My grandmother was a serial divorcer, so "Grampa Bill" wasn't even related to me. He and my grandmother never even legally married. So it would have been enough for him to put up with my shit, but to actively support and encourage the little bastard that made a mess out of his house every day was beyond the call of duty.

Over the years, my mother bought a house and my grandparents upgraded to managing a slightly nicer apartment building, but I never lived too far from them. In fact, when the time came to spread my wings and fly into a place of my own, I gathered up some roommates and we moved into the building my grandparents managed. They were both older at this point, but that didn't stop my grandfather from yard work and general maintenance. What did stop him was a broken hip.

He fell down around the time that my lease was up, so it made good sense for me to surf their couch for a while and make sure everything was okay. Plus, it took a lot of pressure off me. Given that my daily breathing is a crapshoot, it was nice to have a safety net.

It ended up being quite a learning experience for me. It turns out that when they sleep, old people sound exactly like haunted houses. The only thing scarier than the creaks and groans they make is when the noises stop, because you're sure someone just died. Sleeping on the couch was a constant push and pull between "Jesus, I wish that noise would stop!" and "Oh no, I killed them with my thoughts!"

It was also the first time I was ever confronted by grown up math that was flat out wrong. I didn't want to show up and strip anyone of responsibility, so I resisted taking over financial matters. This lasted until I had to give an hour long lecture about subtraction. Our subtraction lesson started with me talking in gentle tones about carrying and things like that, but quickly devolved into me screaming "WHERE THE FUCK DID YOU GET THAT 7? IS THAT A B? THAT'S NOT EVEN A NUMBER!?!" Our lessons about the telephone, the remote control and the television devolved in a similar manner. It sounds harsh, but I assure you my frustration brought them great joy.

I didn't mean anything by it, but I get carried away when I can't find the words that will teach a man to fish. Especially when I told you FOUR FUCKING TIMES THAT YOU DON'T EVER NEED TO TOUCH THAT REMOTE! I learned a lot about patience in that apartment.

My grandfather went downhill quickly. I was used to a certain amount of strange behavior, so the day he got out of bed at 3am and thought the hutch was a wooden urinal that had been installed in the living room while he was sleeping, I didn't think much of it. I just yelled from the couch—"That's not the bathroom!"—and stopped him before he fired.

Then one day he decided to pee in an empty plastic jug. This would have been fine if he were able to get out of bed or at least roll to his side, but since he couldn't do either, he was going to piss straight up into the jug and hope that gravity had no dominion in a plastic jug of pee. I was able to stop him before he went too far. I could do nothing to stop the stroke he was having.

I called 911 and they got him to a hospital. He stabilized, but other than a terrifying two days in which he tried to throw a stove and steal a car, we were never able to bring him back home. I'm not proud of that, because I felt like I owed him much more and because I was not able to honor his final wishes to be brought out in the woods and put down like Old Yeller.

Instead, we had to have him cremated, which he would have hated because it involved paying money for the privilege of dying. My grandmother and I were on the hook for $3,000. Even with the help of some friends, it still came down to either paying for ashes or paying for electricity. I chose life.

Bill would have been fine with that, as he assumed the whole funeral industry was full of crooks anyway. But that did not change the fact that without his check coming in, I would have to start bringing in a lot more money. So, I did what any responsible adult would do: I went to Vegas.

Okay, it's not like it sounds. It was for my stepsister's wedding, so the trip was planned way in advance and was almost expense free on my end. Through some clever maneuvering, I was able to come home with just about the same amount of money I had when I left. The trick is to always be around when family members are winning and run like hell once the tide turns.

After coming home from Vegas, I pretended I knew what I was doing and became acting head of the household. It was an uneasy process and thoroughly uninteresting, so I won't breathlessly recount my job search here (I'll wait until later in the book, when I feel like I have you hooked). However, I was so good at it that my father decided I could easily handle the addition of another member to the house: my aunt.

My "aunt" (not her real name) and my grandmother are the same person separated by about 30 years. This means that when they get along, they get along great; but when things turn south, it's hilariously volatile.

There was plenty of time to observe the dynamics of their relationship, because though we increased our living space by renting a small house and there was a spare bedroom that no one was using, they spent almost every hour of the day in the living room, sitting and sleeping on dueling couches.

I tried my damndest to get someone to move into the spare room. I threatened to give myself a second bedroom. I left the good bed in the spare room and slept on a rollaway. Nothing worked. I offered to add satellite television. Nothing. I figured neither of them wanted to appear selfish by taking their own room.

One day I forgot my phone and ran back into the house. My aunt and grandmother had assumed I left, so I entered a living room whose only occupant was the distant sound of giggling and toilet flushes. That is never a good sign.

Those noises were like a siren song. What horrors would I find? Did someone take a massive toilet-breaking shit? Was someone trying to dispose of a body? The toilet flushed again and my grandmother spoke.

"Do you hear them?"

I spoke.

"What the hell are you doing?"

I wasn't sure I wanted to know, but I had to ask.

My suspicions were confirmed: I didn't want to know. It turns out that no one wanted the spare room because it was haunted. More accurately, the water heater located in the closet was haunted. You could hear the voices of the spirits every time you flushed the toilet. Use of the sinks was fine.

I spent a couple of minutes thinking of a way to explain why the water heater creaked, but my thoughts were interrupted by the realization that I now had two kids, ages 50 and 76.

I lived with them for three stressful years, but I learned a lot in that time. I learned how to calmly make a 911 call when a family member makes a cry for help. I learned that it's hilarious when an elderly mother wakes her daughter by getting in her face and saying "Wake up, bitch." I learned that I make a pretty good referee, though exercising extreme patience feels the same as being dead inside. I learned a lot about how other people see the world and how important it is to talk about our differences and problems without using the words "slut" or "old bitch."

I was never able to successfully explain that the water heater was not haunted and that, even if it was, the toilet wasn't a porcelain Ouija board. I stopped short of referring to charts and graphs, because I knew it was pointless. I was outnumbered by toilet ghosts and their belief was so steadfast that I started to wonder if maybe I was wrong (there's precedent for that).

What I took out of that situation was that it's important to be open to new information. It's perfectly fine to change your mind when you learn something new and you should always be trying to learn something new. Otherwise, you spend your life mistaking the sounds of the world around you for ghosts in the toilet.

~~~~~

We Belong Dead

As a child, I was always scared that when I went to the movies, they'd show the trailer for *Child's Play* and I'd be stuck in a dark theater surrounded by the sights and sounds of the most terrifying film ever made. I was fucking terrified of that doll. It was like Don Mancini went into my head and pulled out my deepest nightmare.

At 5 years old, I was absolutely terrified by the *trailer* to *Child's Play*. What does that say about me? Was there some dark childhood trauma that left scars for that trailer to rip open anew each time it screened?

No, what it says about me is that, before I lost half my stuff in my parent's divorce, I owned a My Little Buddy doll. I mean, sure, we were friends or, more accurately, buddies, but it's not like we were best friends (at that age, my best friend was a stuffed cat named Carmichael). There was something about his wide, dead eyes that I couldn't fully trust. *Child's Play* was confirmation that my little buddy was out to kill me the whole time.

This terror was the beginning of a fascination. I wasn't quite ready to watch them myself, but I was ready to ask various baby sitters a barrage of questions about what horror movies they may have seen and what happened in them (I also thought I was ready to play the *Friday the 13th* Nintendo game, only learning years later than no one is ever really ready to play the *Friday the 13th* Nintendo game, because it's terrible).

Then came the library. It was there, little more than a year removed from the trauma of the *Child's Play* trailer, that I came across the garish orange glory of the Crestwood House Monster Series picture books. As far as I can tell, these books were specifically built to corrupt young minds by interspersing a concise history of the title monster between awesome black and white shots from their filmography.

There were only two of these books at the library and, by lieu of the Dewey Decimal system, I came across *Dracula* first. I don't remember much about the words, but I do remember those beautiful black and white pictures. They burned themselves directly into my cerebral cortex. Even in a loosely bound, beat up children's library book, Bela Lugosi had power and presence and the gothic architecture reminded me of my beloved *Batman*. It was almost enough to snare me in a web of monster fandom. Almost.

The next book I came across, by lieu of the fact that the library only had two monster books, was *Frankenstein*. It was shocking to me, mostly because I felt like someone should have shown me this book sooner. As much as I would love to be a purist about things and ride a "that's not what the monster looked like in the original novel" high horse, Jack Pierce's makeup design handily proves that the source material was flat-out wrong about the design. I could stare at the pictures in that book for hours. Hell, if that book showed up on my desk right now, I'd probably still stare at the pictures for hours. To me, that design will always be Frankenstein's Monster.

Writing about the make-up design with a scholarly detachment makes it seem like I was gently stroking my chin and enjoying a fine chardonnay whilst internally debating the merits of a cotton and collodion applique. I was 6. There was a very, very small part of me that knew I was looking at a man made up to look like a monster, but the rest of me did not give one square inch of fuck. All I saw was a monster. A monster I felt like I knew.

Strangely enough, on the cover of *Frankenstein* the Crestwood House Monster Series used a shot of Lon Chaney, Jr as the monster. The makeup was there, but the face was slightly off. Even in a still picture, you could see something wasn't quite right in the eyes. Much like many have tried to redesign the Monster and come up short, many have played the Monster, but I never believed anyone like I believed Boris Karloff.

Thanks to the fact that the library had a copy of *Frankenstein* on VHS, I saw the movie shortly after reading the book (I wouldn't see *Dracula* until Universal released it on mass market VHS in 1992). Unlike the abject terror I felt when I stared at Chucky, I was never scared of Frankenstein's Monster. I'm surprised anyone ever was. The terror in Frankenstein is not the terror of "Sweet Christ, there's a monster in the village!" Sure, he kills a child, but who hasn't accidentally hurt someone while playing? You did that in a body that you had for years; the Monster only had his body for, at most, a few weeks. How could you expect him to know his own strength? And Fritz? Fuck Fritz. He had it coming. The terror in *Frankenstein* is the Monster's plight. I think if you play that movie for any child under the age of 10, they will immediately see that the Monster just needed a friend. He's angry, sad and confused, all at the same time, and he has no idea how to express it. He's a lumbering monster who should not be alive, but is given breath by science and technology. What is that like? What if you were born wrong?

Yeah, what if?

I was too young to understand everything that happened in my brain when I first watched that movie. In time, it all became clear. I loved Batman when I was younger (and still do today), but that was about transcendence. It was about trying to be something more than I was. The human ideal. *Frankenstein* was about reflection. It was about making peace with who I was and am. It was a thought experiment, an exercise in empathy. And to a much lesser extent, it was about killing hunchbacks.

I've never killed a hunchback but, like the monster, I've often pondered my evolutionary place. I mean, I can't eat and I can't breathe. That's hardly the makings of a successful species. Without modern medicine, I would be a compost heap right now. A very attractive compost heap, but compost nonetheless. I can't ignore that. Modern society doesn't have me outside rustling up some berries before the sun god turns his back to us and plummets us into darkness, but in another time, in another place all I would have required from life was a small plot of land and some potting soil.

As it stands, I'm alive, but it's been very hard to get comfortable with my place in the world. I guess if you step back and think about it, a great number of us are only alive because of science and technology. And many people are too busy to worry about these things because they're more concerned about where their next meal is going to come from. I should probably get over it, but a part of me will always wonder if I am a monster. The rest of me already knows.

~~~~~~

If Nature is so Great, How Come There's Not More of it Inside?

I'm not much of a camper. I don't go to work all week just so I can sleep outside. Even before I worked, I found camping to be disrespectful to the lengths my parents were going to in order to keep a roof over my head. This feeling is apparently not genetic. Or, if it is, it may be a recessive trait. Either way, I've had to do way more camping than I really care for.

Off the top of my head, I can think of three camping trips that my father has taken. All three were to a campground about 6 miles away from where I lived with my mother. It was a much more exotic 30 miles away from my dad's house, so I kind of see how that might seem like a getaway for him, but for me, it was just sleeping at the park. I attempted to go on at least two of those excursions, but once grown-up-drunk-time started, I really started to miss my things. Luckily, my grandparents lived right down the hall from my mother and me, so a phone call was all it took to get my grandfather to come pick me up and reunite me with my beloved Sega Genesis.

My mother, not wanting to sleep at the same park where I decided that team sports were not for me, preferred to vacation in upstate New York, about 4 hours away from our tiny little town of Jewett City, CT. That's fine. She's an independent woman and I continue to support her right to vacation wherever she pleases. However, she expected me to go with her. And by "expected", I mean forced.

That makes it sound much worse than it was, but if she wants to tell her side of the story, she can write her own book.

In the summer of my sixth year, my mother decided we would sacrifice one week of our lives to the forests of Lake George, NY. If this were simply a mother/son trip, I could see why my participation would be required. I wouldn't be happy about it, but I would understand. But she invited friends and her boyfriend and his kid, so I wasn't necessary to the equation. I would have served fine as someone she could look forward to seeing when she got home. She could have showed me pictures and everything. It would have worked out well for both of us.

Instead, I went camping. I was not killed by a bear and I learned about skee ball at an in-town arcade, so the trip wasn't a total wash. My mom took that as a sign that we should do it every year, which I, being of sound mind and body, was staunchly against. I lost that argument, coming out of it with the promise that once I turned 16, I would no longer be forced to camp.

There could be an alternate universe where I realized how valuable that time together was and continued to go on those vacations long past my 16th birthday, but in *this* universe, I was perfectly content to spend time with my mother in the comfort of the shelter she worked so hard to provide me with. Really, my decision was a testament to her hard work. I love you, Mom.

My decision was also a testament to the fact that I was sick of spending time on a filthy men's room floor. No, my mother did not send me there to punish me: Jesus did.

Much like latter day interpretations of Frankenstein's Monster, I need electricity to operate. Being that lightning is never a given and campgrounds are the opposite of electricity-having-places, this led me to the one outlet I could find--in the men's room.

Pulmozyme, the drug that thins out the mucus in my lungs, goes in a nebulizer which is attached to an air compressor. This air compressor does not run on wishes and positive thoughts: it runs on electricity. Though I had a hand-me-down battery powered compressor as well, I could never get it to hold a proper charge. All this, combined with the fact that Pulmozyme requires refrigeration, strikes me as plenty of motivation to live my entire life within a 10 foot radius of a power outlet.

Since I was using my Flutter for airway clearance throughout these camping trips,

Pulmozyme was the only treatment I did that required electricity. So, on average, I only required 10 minutes of electricity a day. Doesn't sound like a lot, does it? In the span of a lifetime, 10 minutes isn't much. But if you spend those 10 minutes in an active men's bathroom, trying your damndest not to touch anything while fielding questions about the bizarre mist producing machine you've introduced to the ecosystem, that 10 minutes feels a lot longer.

For safety purposes, I brought along a friend and/or guardian. In retrospect, I may have found it less stressful to just go by myself, because the only thing more awkward than a scrawny kid smoking Pulmozyme in the men's room is a scrawny kid smoking Pulmozyme in the men's room with an audience.

I don't know how much time you've spent hanging out in campground men's rooms, but the vast majority of them have concrete floors that, through some arcane magic, are able be wet at all times. I guess I could have brought a camping chair in there with me, but at the time, I wanted to be able to make as quick a getaway as possible, so I stood by the door, looking like the world's most bizarre men's room attendant. From this vantage point, I was able to make eye contact with everyone that walked in the door which, being that this was a campground in the height of summer camping season, meant that I got to talk to every drunk that had to piss between 8:10 pm and 8:20 pm. This was often limited to nothing more than a polite "hello", though sometimes they asked the standard questions you would ask of someone who is standing in a bathroom using some kind of smoking machine.

My personal favorite was the guy who came in, nodded "hello" and apparently spent the entire five minutes of his bowel movement thinking about the best way to broach the white elephant in the room. Before stumbling out of the men's room, he looked at me with a chemically induced cross-eyed stare and asked the burning question: "So, uh, do you think I could put some alcohol in that?"

If I had some extra nebulizers, I could have made a killing renting that machine out. It probably would have killed some people too, but I have full confidence that the courts would have recognized the waiver they signed as legally binding.

Natural disasters provide another excellent opportunity for me to remind myself that I run on 120v AC power. The first thing I think of in any power outage is a list of possible areas I can go to curl up with my nebulizer. Luckily, I have a lot of options. I have friends in a variety of areas on a variety of power grids and, if all else fails, my mother owns a generator.

Eventually, I'd like to buy a generator in the shape of a proton pack and strap it to my back so that I'm never too far from power. Or maybe I'll just buy another battery powered compressor. I'm sure the technology is much improved on those. That doesn't mean I'm going to take a chance on camping. I just like to have options. Because no matter what I do, I know the men's room floor is always waiting for me.

~~~~~~

The Ol' CF Luck

In my early years, I struggled a lot with the concept of luck. My grandmother did not. She knew she was lucky. Gram liked the slots quite a bit and spent countless hours and dollars wooing Lady Luck. She was, by her estimation, a gifted slot player and knew exactly how to work the system.

Unfortunately, Gram was not a gifted mathematician. In her mind, losing the money she brought to the casino was breaking even. If at any point during the festivities she had more than the $100 she originally put in the machine, her mind converted the entire amount to profit. This wouldn't be such a terrible thing if she took any of that money out of the machine, but she rarely did. Instead, she would say she won $247 or something, but she "put it all back like a fool ", noting that it was "all their [the casino's] money anyway." I had never questioned it before I lived with her because she was an adult and had earned the right to spend her money however she pleased. I was happy to pretend she knew what she was doing.

She did not.

One day she came home and said "Well, I was up, but I put it all back, so I came home even."

"Gram, just out of curiosity, how much money did you bring to the casino?" I asked.

"One hundred dollars."

"And how much did you bring home?"

"I didn't bring home any."

"So, you lost $100."

"No, I...did I?"

"Yeah Gram, you lost $100."

"What about all that money that I won?"

"Did you bring it home?"

"No."

"Then it doesn't count."

"Well, I lost this time, but I've been lucky before!"

She had brought home money on occasion. However, when we did a little research into her Win/Loss for the year, we found that she was $3000 in the red. She swore she would never go back after that, something she forgot the second she felt lucky again. It took about 3 days.

If I had to pick a point when I decided that luck didn't exist, I would pick that conversation. But life isn't neatly wrapped up in a convenient narrative; this goes much deeper than my grandmother's questionable accounting.

I've long bristled at the idea that I am lucky. It comes up a lot because I am a person with Cystic Fibrosis who is often both alive and not in the hospital. By most metrics, that certainly qualifies as lucky and people will often tell me that I am lucky because they either want to make me feel better or stop hearing about my problems. Sometimes, it's a combination of the two. But if I were really lucky, would I have Cystic Fibrosis at all? Well, I had a 1 in 30,000 chance of getting CF, so I guess that counts as lucky. It was the first and last thing I ever won.

What bothers me about luck is that I feel like it discredits the amount of time and effort that I put into making sure I wake up in the morning. What kind of luck involves the daily beating of mucus from one's bronchial tree, a daily workout regimen and a handful of pills?

The real kind of luck.

To the surprise of no one, my younger self didn't really know what he was talking about. Is there a kind of luck that does not exist? Absolutely. The kind of luck that makes people rub their taint three times while doing the moonwalk in hopes that cosmic forces will smile upon their penny as it scratches off the hot 7s on their $20 lottery ticket does not exist. But if by "luck" you mean that things sometimes go your way, then yes, luck exists.

The concept of luck has become abused and misused. It's human instinct to look at the series of misfortunes that you call a life and assume that someone, somewhere is fucking with you. Likewise, walking through life unscathed while everyone else is cracking under the weight of their burden will easily make one believe that you are a natural born winner. And once that narrative is put in place, it's hard to shake it.

Life involves chance, just not as much as you think. And luck is not a narrative. It is the condition of being placed in a position or situation that required little to no input on your part. Or, as it sometimes goes, it is being placed in a position or situation in spite of the input on your part.

Acquiring Cystic Fibrosis required little to no input on my part. It was just one of those unlucky things that happen. However, there are a number of treatments available to fight the disease. These treatments exist due to little to no input on my part. Getting CF was not a lucky break, but being alive at a time when these treatments exist is. However, even if I keep up with aggressive disease maintenance, there's always a point where my body's impressive mucus production will refuse to be tamed by mere medicine and beatings. That's shitty luck. And it's completely okay to complain about that because it's not my fault. That's the difference between bad luck and poor planning.

For some reason, I cannot shut off the part of my brain dedicated to keeping me from getting stabbed. Normally, this is a good thing. But it's inconvenient when that part of my brain screams "RUN!!" when it's time for any kind of shot or blood work. In fact, when the process of having my blood drawn was explained to me, I decided that if they wanted my blood, they'd have to fight me for it. I was only 6 at the time, so my mother had very little trouble dragging my ass all over the hospital and straight into the phlebotomist's office.

By the time I was a decent match for my mother, my hatred of needles had died down. I wasn't going to start hanging out with needles on the weekends or anything, but I learned to tolerate them in the same way that I tolerate vegetables: I will never actively seek them out, but if they show up, I'll do what I have to. It was a tough lesson to learn.

When I became an "adult," I had some insurance issues and some money issues, so there was a decent stretch of time where I did not keep up on my regularly scheduled doctor visits. Somehow, my brilliant medical mind decided that my normal 3 month interval between check-ups was far too frequent for someone of such sterling physique and exemplary health. An interval of one year was more conducive to my busy schedule of sitting on my ass.

Now, I never stopped with my medications, so I managed to float through much of the year without incident. However, not scheduling an appointment in the fall meant I would be missing a crucial component of my maintenance routine: I would not be getting a flu shot.

I very easily could have gone to the drug store my mother was working at, asked her for $30 and gotten a flu shot right there on the spot. It was within walking distance of my apartment. However, that small part of my brain saw an opportunity to prove to everyone that we didn't require any more shots and quietly filed that information away.

Shockingly, I got the flu that year and I couldn't even complain about it, because it was my own damn fault. It wasn't bad luck, it was dumbassery. Sure, there's a slight chance I would've still gotten it even if I had been properly vaccinated, but one situation is like walking by the hornet's nest and the other is like slapping the hornet's nest with your tits and hoping you don't get stung. I'll let you decide which is which.

If anything, I consider myself pretty lucky to have gotten a very mild case that I was able to sleep off/sweat out in about three days, without having to drag my stubborn ass to a hospital. Looking back on it now, not going to the doctor's for any of this seems insane, but I assure you that it made sense at the time. Maybe that was just the fever talking.

I feel a little guilty that the flu didn't kill me. I feel guilty that a lot of things haven't killed me. I get a little twinge of survivor's guilt every time I hear about someone who is waiting for a lung transplant or had a lung transplant or died from Cystic Fibrosis. There is always a part of me that thinks it should have been me or, at the very least, wonders why it wasn't me. Surely it's not my positive outlook on life, because my positive outlook on life does not exist. I work very hard to keep my lungs clear, but I'm sure there are people who work much harder and feel much worse. I've never been in the hospital for an extended stay, but that probably has more to do with the fact that I tend to keep my mouth shut when I get sick; that should have killed me right there.

There's no mystical force involved. If you'd like to believe there is, then you must also credit that force for killing everyone it didn't save. There's no guardian angel making every cough productive and every scratch off a winner. There's just preparation and chance. And when those things work in your favor, feel free to call them "luck."

If Nature is so Great Part II: Whale Watching

When I was 8 years old, I received a check in the mail. A family had recently lost their child to CF and--as part of the grieving process--sent some money to a few other people with CF. The check came with instructions to use the money towards an experience or to do something fun or something like that. I don't fully remember the contents of the letter. I also don't recall the name of the family. I really wish I did, because it was a fantastically selfless gesture that meant a lot to me both then and now. The details are a little hazy because on that day in 1991, I became rich. I was the only 8 year old I knew with their very own $200 check.

I must have received the check sometime around August, because the second I had that thing in my hand, I knew exactly where it was going: to the local Toys R Us to purchase a Super Nintendo.

This plan had a fatal flaw in that I was 8 years old and had no idea how to cash a check. That meant I'd have to bring a third party into the operation. This story would have a much different ending if my grandmother, who watched me open the letter, was the type of person who had a bank account or drove a car. Since she didn't do either of those things, I had to pass this check off to whoever could get me to the toy store the fastest. That's how my mom entered the scene.

When Mom came home from work, I presented her with the check and the letter and, even though I was pretty tuckered out from all the dancing I did earlier, I still managed to work in a small "I'm rich, I'm rich, I'm rich" dance for her. Then she dropped the bombshell:

"We're going to have to use this for bills, you know."

With those words, all the visions I had of swimming through a pile of money slowly drained away. I wanted to play it cool, but it was obvious that my heart just wasn't into the dance anymore.

"Oh yeah, I know, I was just...um...kind of excited to see my name on a check."

Being a single mother is hard enough, so I understand and respect the pressure my mother faced, especially when you threw all the medical bills on top of that. I could not at the time and would not now fault her if she used the check for bills. I love my mother. I just really, really wanted that Super Nintendo.

Luckily, there is a major difference between my mother and myself. If you send me a check, I will cash it. If you send my mother a check, she will call you to question why she has this check and what she should do with it. So, my mother called the doctor's office that facilitated this transaction and asked all the pertinent questions. They told her that she wouldn't have to worry about the bills and we should use the money for something fun. Super Nintendo, here I come! Then just as the money pool in my head was filling up again, she dropped another bombshell:

"We need to use this money for something fun."

Now, it's tough to convey the tone of this sentence, but I can assure you that every inflection in her voice pointed to me not getting a Super Nintendo.

Instead, it was decided that we would go whale watching out on Cape Cod. I don't remember exactly how this was decided. It may have been that I was so downtrodden that I just agreed to the first thing that she said. Really, I don't care for boats, the ocean or whales very much. I like lobster though. I probably assumed that we would be eating lobster up there.

We did not eat lobster. We did, however, walk out of a restaurant because I, an 8 year old who thought $200 put him on easy street, noticed the pasta should have come with a payment plan. We also got on a cold boat in rough seas and watched exactly zero whales. Since the boat was never going to turn into Bowser's Castle, I was always bound to be disappointed, but when I saw my mother's face, I knew the truth: this trip really and truly sucked.

They gave us a rain check, but we knew damn well we weren't going back. And though I did not eat any lobster, my mom did buy me a small plush lobster, so the trip wasn't a total bust (full disclosure: I loved that plush lobster with all my heart). And, taking advantage of the broken home rule, I eventually convinced my dad to buy me a Super Nintendo. I was very lucky in that I had both a mother who tried to broaden my horizons and a father who gave me the means to spend a solid 3 and a half years playing *Street Fighter II*. I guess the lesson here though is that it's important to try new things, if only to prove that you were right all along. Hell, even if you do end up enjoying something, you never have to admit it. That way you can have fun and still be right. It's the best of both worlds.

~~~~~

Terminal Illness

There's an old joke where a man sits at a bar, looks at the bartender and says "You see that fence over there? I built that fence with my own two hands. But do they call me McGregor, the fence builder? No. And this bar, I built this bar too, but do they call me McGregor, the bar builder? Nooo! But you fuck one goat…"

Having a terminal illness is a lot like fucking a goat in that it defines you. The words "terminal" and "illness", when used in conjunction, represent a huge concept and, to many people, your life exists in its shadow. They are towering, cold and official.

I hate them. I hate those words: terminal illness.

Unfortunately, the words "terminal illness" are very useful in describing a terminal illness. As much as those words reek of euphemistic emptiness, the alternatives—fatal disease, lethal sickness, incurable complaint—all sound like late 80s thrash bands. So, no matter how much fun I try to have with the fact that my body is slowly telling me to go fuck myself, it still comes down to those two words: terminal illness.

It's always awkward when terminal illness enters the conversation. I have few qualms about being viewed as a human oddity, but people often feel like I do and think I'm lying if I tell them I don't. A lot of people will apologize for the illness, which is nice, but it's not their fault. Truthfully, I'd prefer $10 to an apology, but I can't expect them to take that much responsibility for something they had nothing to do with.

While they may not have money for me, they often have questions and I'm happy to answer them. They usually tap dance around the topic at first, but once they start to believe I'm comfortable with it, they'll at least pretend to be comfortable as well, so it works out. I can't expect their comfort level to immediately match mine; it's a big concept and I've been dealing with it for 30 years. These things take time.

I don't have time, so I try to drag them into comfort as quickly as possible. I knew my fiancée for 2 hours before I brought up Cystic Fibrosis. And by "knew", I mean "had typed a few words out to her on a dating website." Should I have waited a while and broken the news to her after we had actually met? Well, that's one way to do it, but I think my results speak for themselves.

Strangely enough, I think my comfort with the disease made it harder for her to find her place with it. Before I joined forces with Bekka, I spent about 4 years by myself, which was a great way for me to figure out how to deal with CF in my adult life. I learned a lot about how to listen to my body, but jack shit about how to communicate what's happening to my body. That was a learning process for both of us (there's a reason this book was written AFTER I had met Bekka).

'Twas a snowy night in November and we were doing some grocery shopping. I hadn't been feeling great, but I'm used to not feeling great, so I went anyway. Somewhere, between the soft drinks and the produce, my chest got really tight. Normally, I'd take a hit of albuterol and sit down for a little while, but I left the albuterol at home and I didn't want to abandon the shopping, so I decided to just push through it. Not wanting to impede Bekka's shopping experience, I didn't say anything about it.

It didn't get better, so by the end of our nacho gathering sojourn, my lungs felt 3 sizes too small. When we were finally in the car, I announced that my chest felt a little tight. She was concerned, but it wasn't until we got home that she realized I am a master of understatement. She was not amused.

She was very angry with me for not telling her what was going on, as she should have been. Since there was really nothing I could do to fix it at the time, I figured it didn't make any sense to announce it. It was my problem and I was going to have to deal with it. But, as she said, I would feel terrible if something was wrong with her and she didn't tell me immediately.

It's not that I want to face every challenge with a stoic grace, it's just that I'm used to not saying anything. My body is like a crappy car that I'm used to driving. Every once in a while it does something and everyone else is like "What the fuck was that!?!", but I just give it a swift kick and get on my way. There's a lot wrong with it, but I've grown comfortable in the old jalopy.

However, I do not want anyone to mistake that comfort for bravery. I feel like bravery implies that you had a choice and you took the courageous path. I don't have a choice. If I did, you can be damn sure that CF would not be that choice. I'm sure it's possible to face these challenges with bravery and grace, but I never cared to try it myself.

I've also never viewed it as a test. I know some people do. Those people may actually be brave. I am not one of those people. I've learned from CF but I'm sure that the world could have found another way to teach me how to take pills. Maybe an episode of Fat Albert or something. If this is a test, it sucks and if it's part of some divine plan, that plan sucks too. But, I deal with it, because I don't have a choice.

My fiancée, Bekka, does have a choice or so it seems. As far as I know, she is not with me through some companionship program for respirationally deficient individuals (that's the preferred term for Cystic Fibrosis patients) but I've never come out and asked her either (update: she is not). However, she tells me she is often lauded for the strength she shows in donating her time to me. It probably doesn't come out exactly like that, but that's the gist of it.

Again, people assume that she's engaged to the concept of "terminal illness" and that every day represents a delicate balance of harrowing tragedy and fleeting triumph. Sure, if you had to deal with everything CF had to throw at you all at once, it would be overwhelming, however when distributed out over time, it feels mostly like a lot of coughing and farting. And the more you're exposed to both the CF and the farts, the more they just start to feel normal. Sure there are times when it gets scary and she certainly worries about me quite a bit (I am, after all, a precious bundle of joy), but a good portion of our daily turbulence comes straight out of my ass.

She puts up with it though and she puts up with all the non-medical stuff too, because, well, what can you do? That's what love is: putting up with another person until they finally die. The candle that burns half as long is twice the pain in the ass.

Seriously though, while "terminal illness" is a huge concept, the various machinations of daily life don't give one square fuck about it. Bills still show up, the laundry still has to get done and you may or may not be able to breathe while you do it. You just try to do as much as you can for as long as you can do it and hope that it's enough. If not, don't worry. You'll be dead soon anyway.

~~~~~

McPizza

As a child, I was an easy mark for advertisements. As proof of this, I offer the fact that I've eaten more than one McDonald's Pizza. If you don't remember McDonald's Pizza, that's because it didn't last long. This was a personal pan pizza that took 10 minutes to cook, served at a place well known for making burgers happen to you in about a minute. It was obviously a product that wouldn't be around forever.

Though they seem to have been test marketed as early as 1989, these pizzas came to my area—Southeastern Connecticut—sometime around 1993/94. My chronology may be off, but whenever it was, I assure you that during that time, pizza was the only thing I ate at McDonald's. I don't know why I ate so many of them. Maybe I saw a little bit of myself in that pizza. Maybe I felt bad for the guy who was going to be fired for coming up with the idea. More likely, I just really liked pizza, even if the cheese was hotter than a thousand suns and took roughly 20 minutes to cool off. It made me feel like a Ninja Turtle.

My father indulged this need for fast food pizza, which I respect, because I would have told me to go fuck myself. I don't even remember an audible sigh when he asked what I wanted and I said "Pizza!" Maybe he always assumed this time would be different. More likely, he just didn't care.

A 10 minute wait inside the restaurant isn't much of a problem. There are seats and everyone else in your party can enjoy their food while you wait for your damn pizza. At the drive thru, it was different. If you ordered the pizza, they'd check to see if they had one made, which I'm pretty sure was just a show, because they never did. Instead, they'd ask you to pull up a little to let the other cars through and, upon its completion, someone would hand deliver your pizza.

At this point, most people would say "Fuck the pizza, just give me some nuggets", but at the age of 11, pizza was a top priority in my life. I didn't even care about the other people in the car; as far as I was concerned, they fucked up by not ordering pizza too. Yes, there was a time when I felt that not ordering McDonald's Pizza was a mistake. Of course, if everyone did it, I'd probably think it had gone mainstream and switched to the Filet-o-Fish or something.

Anyway, one fateful Saturday, my father took my friend Anthony, my half-brother Jake and myself to McDonald's and, as always, I ordered the pizza. Wisely not wanting to take baby Jake into the restaurant, we used the drive thru. After the drive thru attendant performed the standard show of checking to see if a pizza was available, my father was instructed to pull up to the curb; someone would deliver our pizza as soon as it was ready.

This was to be an uneventful Saturday afternoon trip, but the lady in the car behind us spiced things up by honking at my father. Now, though my father drove a behemoth of an Oldsmobile, he had given plenty of room for things to carry on as usual for everyone in line behind us. This lady could easily drive around our car and enjoy her two all-beef patties. Instead, possibly assuming that we had completely forgotten how a drive-thru worked, she honked at us. My father, his patience already tested by the pizza, did not handle this well.

"What the fuck is she honking at?" he muttered as he stuck his arm out of the window and indicated that the woman should drive around. After she figured out how to turn her car to the right, she parked in the lot and began to enjoy her meal. Within a minute or so, my pizza was delivered and we were set to go home, but my father couldn't properly enjoy his meal until he took care of some unfinished business.

He pulled into a parking spot one car length away from the lady honker. He rolled down the passenger window and indicated that she should roll down her driver side window so that they might have a discussion. I was in the back seat at the time, so I'm not sure how the second side of the conversation went, but I could see what was happening and I heard my father's side loud and clear. He opened up with:

"What the fuck is your problem?"

pause

"They told me to park there, you stupid bitch!"

pause

At this point, a gentleman in the other car leans forward to defend the woman.

"Who the fuck are you?"

pause

"How old are you, 14? Get out of the car, I'm going to kick your fucking ass!"

Oh, how I hoped for that ass kicking. How often do you get to see your father kick a teenager's ass over a pizza in a McDonald's parking lot? Not often enough.

Unfortunately, almost immediately after the words came out of his mouth, my father thought better of it. He screamed, "Fuck it, it's not worth it" and we left. He didn't let the anger take complete hold of him, because he thought about the consequences. That's not to say he didn't fish tail out onto route 12 with his middle finger extended, but he still drove away.

Often, when I tell people that anger is a good thing, they immediately think I'm referring to the type of anger that makes you have to explain to three different mothers and various law enforcement officials why you just kicked a teenager's ass in front of three minors in a McDonald's parking lot. Amusing though it may be, this anger is mostly useless. Anger directed towards people often is. But anger always comes from passion and if you can direct that in the right place, you can make some real changes. You just need to be sure you're mad at the right thing.

What was the real problem in this situation? It wasn't the lady honking her horn; she was confused and scared. There's no need to be angry at her. It wasn't my father either; he was just defending his ground. Personally, I blame the pizza. Not me for ordering it and not the workers who, I'm sure, did the best they could with the situation. It was the pizza and the entire corporate structure that thought waiting 10 minutes for a pizza was still well within the definition of "fast" food. We shouldn't settle for that and we didn't. That pizza told us to pull up to the curb and we told it to go fuck itself. Slowly, it disappeared. I'm sure everyone involved had the best intentions, but the idea was simply toxic and needed to be killed. It was and no one was hurt.

Anger, like gasoline, can be used as fuel, but if you start throwing it around all willy nilly, you're bound to burn something down. It's okay to be angry as long as you know when, where and how to use it.

The more you know.

Woooooo!

Growing up, I thought everyone had fucked up fingers. Mine, of course, were a model of anatomic perfection. Was everyone else putting antifreeze on their Coco Puffs? How did they end up with such strangely shaped fingers?

Along with Cystic Fibrosis, I was also born with a terminal case of "Fuck Everyone Else's Noise." I went to the doctor's office every three months and every three months, the doctor would ask me to place my thumbs back to back with my knuckles lined up and the nails touching. I would later find out that this was called Schamroth's Test and was used to check for a small, diamond shaped opening that should be present when your nails are placed together. If your fingers look more like E.T.'s and no window is present, you have clubbed fingers.

Clubbed fingers are usually a symptom of lung or heart disease, so it makes perfect sense that I have them, but I was young and in complete denial about the possibility that anything could be even remotely wrong with my fingers. Weren't the lung problems enough? I just thought the doctor was checking to see if that little bump right below my nail was swollen. I don't know what swollen nail bumps mean, but that amount of denial is probably the sign of a larger problem.

In my defense, being an only child at the time meant that I didn't have contact with a lot of peer fingers. Everything I knew about how fingers looked was gleaned from my parents and television. Even when I did play with friends or disembodied hands, it wasn't like we were comparing manicures. I had a solid foundation on which to build the belief that my fingers were a perfectly normal example of little kid digits. I figured that when I grew up, they would somehow morph into the adult sized monstrosities my parents were sporting. Puberty meant your balls dropped and your fingers turned weird.

I'd love to say that I abandoned this belief immediately upon entering the public school system, but you would be surprised at how long a shitty belief can stand when built on a foundation of ignorance. Even though I was now sitting in close quarters with a bunch of fingers trying to borrow my scissors and steal my paste, I maintained steadfast dedication to the idea that every one of these kids was a goddamn freak. The worst part is that my sample size was huge: between kindergarten and third grade, I attended three different schools, each at least 30 miles apart from the previous. The only slight credit I can give myself is that one of these schools had kids so ugly, the idea of a tainted water supply producing an entire generation of freaks was not totally out of the question.

As much as I had silently judged their digits, no one ever brought up the unique qualities of my fingers. Maybe they were living in similar finger ignorance or "fingnorance" bubbles. Maybe they were just polite. Maybe, and this is a long shot, most kids don't take a moment each day to catalog the types of fingers they see around them.

My fingnorance continued unabated until April 5, 1992. By this time, I was in third grade and I had a lot of experience sharing tables and pencils and snack foods with all kinds of germy little fingers, so the foundation was beginning to crack. But it wasn't until that fateful Sunday, watching the *Wrestlemania VIII* Pay-Per-View preview, seeing Ric Flair point at the screen as he explained to Mean Gene Okerlund that he had carnal knowledge of the Macho Man's wife, that something went wrong in my head.

"Look at those fingers. They look like everyone else's fingers. But that can't be possible! Ric Flair is the Nature Boy, so by definition, he should be a perfect example of…oh god. No…no….NOOOOO!"

As much as I had tried to emulate Batman when I was younger, I was not the World's Greatest Detective.

I processed this new knowledge very quickly, quietly thanking myself for having never vocalized these concerns to anyone and deciding to pass it off like I had always known I had freak fingers. These days, I will occasionally mention that I am self-conscious about it, but that's just a ruse to distract your attention from my tiny, velociraptor-style wrists. I take some comfort in the fact that I have always known that my wrists were strange, a conclusion I came to without the help of any wrestling superstars.

However, do not think for a moment that I didn't start an all Slim Jim diet the second I saw those Macho Man commercials.

~~~~~~

The Fun of Failure

I sucked at the very first thing I ever attempted. Granted, if what I've learned from TV is true, most newborns aren't great at breathing, but a slap on the ass seems to fix it. You could slap my ass for three days straight and I'm still not going to win any trophies for breathing. Hell, there are some mornings it feels like I've forgotten how to breathe. If it's true that you learn more from failure than from success, then I should be fucking brilliant by now. Maybe I'm just a slow learner.

Along with breathing, I've never been great at gaining weight. Thanks to my inefficient physiology, I burn a decent number of calories by simply existing and,thanks to my shitty pancreas, I have a hell of a time replacing those calories. So, for most of my life, my entire body mass consisted of bones, skin and mucus. This bothered me to the point where, just to add some meat to my bones, I would eat until I could feel the food trying to climb back up my esophagus. It was a kind of reverse bulimia, where I binged and spent hours trying really hard not to throw up. And if I happened to toss my cookies, it would be right back to the kitchen for another pound of bacon and half a gallon of milk.

Despite all that bacon, around the age of 20, I was 5'9" (and three quarters!) and 135 pounds. That's not a lot of pounds and, since I have a thin frame, it was incredibly obvious. So, I decided to do something about it.

This "something" was to take a trip to the local sports nutrition store and pick up a tub of their finest weight gain powder (or, at least, the finest weight gain powder that $20 would buy me). The label said to mix four scoops of powder with 16 ounces of water. I, assuming those instructions were just a ploy to get me to buy more weight gain powder, decided to mix four scoops of powder with 16 ounces of half and half. I congratulated myself on this brilliant solution and prepared to gain at least 100 pounds, all while wondering why I had never thought of this before.

I don't know if you've ever taken a big sip of half and half, but it is *thick*. Just drinking 16 ounces of it will give you about one third of the calories you need for the day and a solid 173% of the saturated fat you're looking for. Adding four scoops of weight gain powder gave me a drink with around 1300 calories, 60 grams of fat and 136 carbohydrates. That's about two meals worth of nutrition, and I use that term very loosely, in one hearty snack.

Using the word "drink" in that last paragraph is a bit of a misnomer. I would hesitate to call the product of this union a liquid; it was more of a sludge or a slurry.

Being that half and half is already pretty thick, it doesn't mix well. I thought I had circumvented this problem by using a blender, but that just seemed to piss it off. After about three minutes of futile blending, what I ended up with was a thick cream base with some delightful powder clump suspensions floating through it. After making careful note of the insolubility of the weight gain powder, I did the only reasonable thing: I drank it anyway. Even though I had to chew through most of it, the taste wasn't nearly as offensive as I had imagined. In fact, I was still in good enough spirits that I was able to knock back a plate of Swedish meatballs afterward.

Over the next two days, I managed to repeat that process three times. By the third meal, the novelty had gone. My body was fighting that slurry the whole way down and I was choking back my follow up frozen dinner with a funereal sense of purpose. But, having learned years ago to not take shit from my body, I managed to make it all disappear. Given the amount of effort required to both ingest and process, it should come as no surprise that I fell asleep soon after.

It was a bit of a surprise to me, though. I don't fully remember going to bed, so I woke up in a haze around 9:45pm. Since I had to be to work at 11pm, I skipped my meal in favor of doing my breathing treatments and then slowly shuffled myself to the car. I didn't really feel like eating, but since I was determined to gain weight, I lied to myself and said I would scrounge up a meal at work.

I worked the Night Audit shift at a local hotel, which is a sweet job if you don't mind the hours. Nothing happens and for long stretches of time I was the only employee in the building. Friends would often stop in on their way home from their jobs/night time activities and we'd talk while waiting for some drunks to stumble in looking for rooms. On this particular night, my friend Mike had stopped in to talk comic books and related items. At least that's what I think he was talking about. He very well could have been giving a socio-economic analysis of the European Union. My body had diverted energy from all non-essential function and channeled it to the two most important tasks: digestion and sweating. Given that my body isn't great at digestion anyway, it felt like someone had converted my stomach into a high volume meth lab. Maybe that's why I was sweating so much; my stomach knew the end was near. Not wanting to leave the desk for too long, I thought I could hold in whatever was happening, but nature was not calling: nature had a warrant and was about to break down the door. The time was now. I put up a sign that said "Be Back in 5

Minutes", jumped the desk and ran to the bathroom.

Once my ass hit the porcelain, things got ugly. I would have sworn that I was passing a slightly premature child out of my asshole. My legs were off the ground and I'm pretty sure I put claw marks in the bowl. I'd love to pretend that it mattered to me if people could hear the screams coming from the bathroom, but every shit I could give was plopping straight into the bowl below me.

After about three minutes of pushing out the produce, it was over. I took a courtesy wipe of my ass, but it only confirmed what I already knew: this shit was solid and, much like a courteous hiker, had left no trace. The only thing to left to do was to get up and admire my handiwork.

At this point, I'll note that I have very tiny ears. You may be wondering what that has to do with anything and I'll tell you: I think I look pretty cool with a pen behind my ears. Having long hair enabled me to live my lifelong dream of holding a pen behind my ear, but that ear to pen relationship was always tenuous. I know this seems like an odd aside, but when I got up and cast my eyes upon the pile of pain I brought to that toilet—the pile that had banished all the water, save for a small oasis preserved just left of center—I should not have been surprised when I saw a pen tumble onto the top of Mt. Flushmore. However, so rarely do you see a pen in a toilet, that I was a little shocked. I briefly wondered if I should fix that but, as in most times of trauma, instinct took over and I just started flushing. Of course, the first flush did little more than move some water around, so I could have taken a moment there or between one of the other six flushes to do something about the pen, but I assumed the problem would solve itself.

    The problem went away for about 7 and a half hours. I stayed a little late to finish a few things, so I was there when one of the housekeepers ran out of the bathroom screaming "I swear I just peed and now it's green and there's a pen!" The turd had returned, Hulk green with rage, and it brought the pen with it. Feeling some sense of responsibility, I plunged it away. It must have felt some separation anxiety, because after I left, it came back. The manager eventually had to call a plumber and pay him $240 to flush away my creation. Luckily, the bathroom was in a public area and could easily be blamed on a guest. It turns out that in the battle of mind over matter, matter will eventually win—particularly if it is fecal.

    As much as I'd like to pretend that the weight gain mixture detailed above represented a massive shift in my eating habits, it was more of a logical conclusion.

In order to just maintain my weight, I was still eating about 3000 calories a day and dutifully depositing most of those calories in the toilet. I moved from drinking a gallon of whole milk every day to enjoying half and half with a pound of bacon for breakfast. It didn't matter, that weight wasn't going on. I kept trying, but nothing seemed to work.

Once it got warm out and dairy became a less attractive option, I sustained myself on fruit juice and root beer. It seemed like drinking root beer just made me even thirstier than I was when I started; I had no idea that most people didn't drink 6 cans in one sitting. 72 ounces of root beer did a decent job of filling my stomach, but since I didn't have all the calories I needed, I started to add ice cream to it. This didn't help me gain any weight, but it did have the delightful side effect of making my poops smell like expired cookies.

Fruit juice, while delicious, made my pulse fire off like a black market AK-47 and made my head feel like Jesus was pissing directly into my skull. I, of course, assumed that my body had really taken to the taste of Chicken McNuggets and decided to become allergic to fruit. I did not test this theory by trying any actual fruit, but it sounded like solid science to me. Also, it did not stop me from drinking delicious grape juice; I just had to make sure I had plenty of time to lie down afterward.

So I was failing to gain weight, failing to maintain weight and even failing to drink juice. But what did I learn from all this failure? Well, what I learned is that I had diabetes. Those expired cookie poops were not a delightful side effect of my increased float intake: they were a sign that sugar was just passing through my body without a care in the world. This also helped to explain why my pee smelled like Cap'n Crunch—it pretty much *was* Cap'n Crunch.

I had been warned that the scarring on my pancreas would eventually manifest as Cystic Fibrosis Related Diabetes, but I ignored these warnings because I hate needles. However, with encouragement (and a free lunch) from my mommy, I was able to endure the glucose test required to confirm the suspicions that my pancreas is terrible at everything. After all I had been through, after all I had overcome, this was easily the worst thing that had ever happened to me. Not because of the needles or the extra maintenance or the new medications--they were a minor inconvenience at best. They were nothing compared to a lifetime of diet soda.

At least that's how it felt at the time. Though I called bullshit on everyone who said "Oh, you'll get used to it", they were right. I eventually got used to diet soda. And I did it through failure. I meant to buy a diet root beer, but mistakenly came home with a diet cream soda instead. Being too lazy to go back to the store, I drank it anyway. It wasn't bad. In fact, the next time I went to the store, I bought another one.

Many of you right now may be thinking "Why the fuck is he talking about soda?" The truth is, transitions are never easy, even the small ones. In fact, I find the small ones especially hard, because I feel like I should have a choice in the matter. But it's okay if you don't get them right the first time, as long as you never stop trying. I hate needles, so the first time I tried to check my own blood sugar, my hands got so sweaty that the blood went everywhere but the meter. I eventually had a long heart-to-heart talk with needles, we came to an understanding and I tried again. Then I tried a few more times. Then I tried to sneak up on my hand. After much trial and error, I can now use a very tiny needle to poke a very tiny hole in my hand without much panic (in my defense, a big part of the problem was that the original lancing device I had resembled a GI Joe accessory that had been retrofitted for needles).

If you ever plan on living, you'll meet failure. Get to know it. Welcome it in, offer it a cookie, put on a pot of tea and make peace with it. You don't have to be afraid of it. There are people in the world who would kill for just the chance to fail at the thing you just fucked up. So try it again. Find out what went wrong and make your adjustments. Talk about it. Maybe you can learn from other people's mistakes too. I tend to find the mistakes more interesting anyway. Maybe you do too. If not, perhaps you'd be interested in my follow up book, *10 Things I'm Fucking Awesome At*.

    No? Eh, I figured it was worth a shot.

~~~~~

Cultural Cachet

Without looking it up on the internet, tell me Superman's origin. Can you name any of his powers? What about his weaknesses? Who is his girlfriend/wife?

You probably did a pretty good job of answering those questions. But what if I asked you to recall your favorite Superman story? You may not have one. You may have never read a Superman comic or watched a Superman movie. It's perfectly possible that you have no first hand experience with Superman and all your information was gained through second hand sources. It's like cultural diffusion has passed the answer right into your brain.

Now let's take the same questions and substitute Swamp Thing for Superman. How does that affect your ability to answer them?

Since this is a book and I can't hear you answer the questions, I'm going to assume that most of you didn't do so well on the Swamp Thing portion of the test. Maybe you recognize the name, but you draw a blank on the rest. Perhaps this is the first you've heard of Swamp Thing.

Swamp Thing isn't exactly an underground character. He has two movies, a live action tv show, a children's cartoon, a toy line, two video games and a pile of comics under his belt. Granted, it's no match for the avalanche of Superman material, but it's not an insignificant amount. And not all of it is great, but Superman has shown up in his fair share of bullshit as well. No matter how crappy those Swamp Thing video games are, it still doesn't change the fact that Alan Moore's run on the character is one of the finest collections of comics you will ever read. It may not have the cultural cachet of Superman, but it's still a very important part of many people's lives.

Cystic Fibrosis is the Swamp Thing of diseases.

Sure, people may have heard the name; it's out there. It shows up in news every once and a while. Sometimes you'll see a pin or a ribbon for it. But how many people know what it affects? Can they name the symptoms? Do they know the treatment?

What about diabetes?

Diabetes has cultural cachet. People know about diabetes. They know people with diabetes. And if they keep eating like they do, someday they'll have diabetes. That's a disease that plays all the way back to the cheap seats.

That makes diabetes much easier to talk about. If you tell someone you wanted to have a Butterfinger, but you're worried about spiking your sugar, they'll fist bump you and say they feel your pain. Tell them you're concerned about the amount of ozone in the air and they'll just think you're being a pussy.

Having both diseases, I've noticed the disparity (granted, my diabetes is Cystic Fibrosis-related, but to the outside observer, it's functionally equivalent). I'm always dealing with some, to use the technical term, goddamn lung bullshit. My chest is tight, I'm not producing any mucus, I'm producing too much mucus, I need to lie down for a second, on and on. These things require a lot of attention and adjustment and I'm not even taking into account all the digestive problems I have. Diabetes, on the other hand, simply means that I can no longer sit down to a nice bag of Sour Patch Kids. I can have a handful, but if I do, I need to take a couple of small pills to tell my pancreas to make some more insulin. Sometimes the pills work too well and I have to eat a couple more Sour Patch Kids to even things out. Sometimes I don't take enough of the pills and my sugar goes high. Most of the time, I just don't eat any Sour Patch Kids. Once you cut back on sugar, you kind of lose your taste for it.

But while my day is pretty much breathe, breathe, shit, breathe, shit, I spend more time talking about diabetes than I do about Cystic Fibrosis. It comes up a lot. People see you stab your finger. They offer you a dessert you can't eat. They find you passed out, face down, riding a sugar high. More importantly, they already know a little about it, so they have an entrance point. I've noticed a stunning number of people have diabetes, so there's some common ground. It gets complicated once they ask if I have Type 1 or Type 2 and I have to explain that my diabetes is because my pancreas is a free loader who won't do anything unless I spot him a handful of pills, but until then it's smooth sailing.

Having dealt with CF for so long, I tend to talk about it in the same way that you would tell someone about a hidden talent. Due to this, some people will just pretend they have some clue about what I just said. With the shoe on the other foot, that's exactly how I would handle the situation. I'd nod my head and check Wikipedia as soon as I could, possibly while still having the conversation. I find it helps keep the momentum.

Other people have a lot of questions, which I try to answer as well as possible. It's tough because there's a fine line between giving pertinent information and whining. I think no matter what I'm saying, it's coming off as "Um, excuse me, I have a lung disease!". That makes me want to punch myself in the face.

It's not like I don't want people to know I have CF; if I didn't, this book would be a terrible idea. I don't want CF to define me as a person, but if I ever went on the lam, I wouldn't be offended if my description went "Male, brown hair, blue eyes, around 5'9", has Cystic Fibrosis." My problem is that if I'm going to shoehorn something into a conversation, I'd much prefer to go with Swamp Thing (see above). This means I've missed out on 30 years of learning how to talk about Cystic Fibrosis. This book is my attempt at making up for lost time. It's probably too late to turn CF into the Superman of diseases, but I hold out hope that it might become like the Daredevil of diseases.

Law of Limitations

I often use stairs to gauge how I feel. If I am able to pounce up them like a lithe jungle cat, I'm in pretty good health. If I'm more like a spry senior trying to prove he's still got it, it might be time for a little extra airway clearance, but it's not anything to worry about. Once I've decided that all the stairs of the world are part of some vast global conspiracy to keep me on the first floor of things, it's probably time to worry. Usually, I won't notice right away, because I'm angrily trying to prove my superiority to the stairs.

I hate to admit I'm sick. Part of it is a mind over matter thing, but the other part of it is because I often don't want to admit to the prevalence of CF in my life.

In the 1966 book *Psychology of Science*, Abraham Maslow sums up the law of the instruments with this quote: "I suppose it is tempting, if the only tool you have is a hammer, to treat everything as if it were a nail." I think that's a brilliant way of demonstrating how having one central thing in your life alters your vision of everything else. So, I've blatantly ripped that off with my own law of limitations: "When you have a major affliction, it's easy to treat all your problems like limitations."

To avoid blaming CF for everything, I overcompensate by blaming it for nothing. I don't want to give it any power in my life. It makes me feel like it's winning.

Admitting you have limits is a tough thing. Teachers and Parents often say that you can do anything but that's a little overzealous. There are some things that you flat out cannot accomplish. There are other things that you just don't feel like doing. I, for example, will probably never be a world class gymnast, because I'm quite possibly the least flexible human being in the history of the world. But that doesn't mean I couldn't take a shot at it. I could wake up every morning and stretch while thinking of ways to choreograph a killer floor routine to Strapping Young Lad's "Oh My Fucking God." However, I have neither the drive nor the passion to dedicate any amount of time to that, especially after finding out that Men's floor routines are not performed to music. I could learn some gymnastic skills, but I will never be a gymnast.

Notice that nowhere in there did I mention Cystic Fibrosis as being one of the limiting factors crushing my gymnastic dreams. That's because, at this point in my life, it wouldn't stop me from flipping around incessantly. It makes exercise more difficult, but it definitely doesn't make it impossible. If anything, exercise improves my lung function, so I should do as much of it as possible.

But go back and replace the word "gymnast" with "competitive smoker" and we'll see a different story. While I could make an attempt at being a world class competitive smoker, CF would definitely stop me from reaching the top echelon of the sport (I had originally included a joke about how competitive smoking is not a thing, but an internet search proved me woefully wrong). I am confident in pronouncing to the world that Cystic Fibrosis has prevented me from becoming a world class smoker. Heartbreaking, isn't it?

I'll never live off the grid and get back to nature either, because Pulmozyme doesn't grow in the forest and you can't run a nebulizer on tree sap. You want to know what I'd do if the zombie apocalypse comes? Die. I'll fucking die. Then when I become a zombie, I'll die again because I can't digest any of the stragglers I've eaten. I'll be the only zombie trying to break into the pharmacy to see if they have any enzymes left.

Those are extreme examples, so it is easy to see why they're out of reach for me. Most of the limitations of CF are smaller than those: the summer feels like it was actively designed to exterminate me, my lungs act like flypaper for infection and particulates, any job without insurance is essentially useless to me, etc. However, these things become bigger problems when they are ignored. Sometimes, you don't even have to ignore them; they'll become a big problem all by themselves. These things are harder for me to explain to an observer without feeling like I'm giving in or that I've let CF make the decisions in my life.

But it kind of does. It certainly doesn't make all the decisions, but there's no amount of determination that can propel you up the stairs when your lungs begin to act as a bacterial growth hostel. Thankfully, Augmentin and Bactrim do work. I'm sure there are a number of other fine antibiotics, but those are my favorites. I just have to remember to ask for 'em.

~~~~~

Coping

In 1990, the members of Judas Priest went to trial over a case of two boys who tried to kill themselves after listening to the *Stained Class* album. The boys listened to a song called "Better by You, Better Than Me" over and over again for hours then took a shotgun and tried to end their lives. One was successful; one was not. The trial was based on the idea that there were subliminal messages in the music that could only be heard clearly when played in reverse. In particular, the prosecution focused on a vocal part that sounded like it said "Do it!" when played backwards. Certainly, if your brain is primed to hear "Do it!" it's in there, but as the judge pointed out, it's lacking the critical definition of what "it" is. Also, it's backwards. If backwards messaging worked, wouldn't people use it to rob banks?

I'm fascinated by the case, both because of my love of Judas Priest and my interest in facial reconstruction. Certainly, the fact that one young man lost his life and the other lost his face is a tragedy, but whatever made these boys think suicide was a good idea, it probably wasn't Judas Priest. Suing the band was just a way to ignore the actual issue, whatever that may be, while still pretending to address it. The parents did not understand the music, but surely their grief was deep and they should not be demonized for this.

Blaming popular music for real world problems was hot back in the 90s. Later, video games got the blame because, well, what else could it be? These critiques have always been hollow to me, but I think the simplicity is what makes them easy to sell. If we are to believe every sensationalistic media frenzy that implicates some piece of art, culture or, less charitably, product as the downfall of an individual, we also need to account for the number of people that they have saved. "Teenager Decides Not to Kill Himself; Listens to Metal Instead" just doesn't have that ring to it. "Child Plays Violent First Person Shooting Game; Mods Game to Include New Levels and Characters" just doesn't get the clicks that "Call of Duty Killer!!" generates.

I'm a decade removed from the tail end of my teenage years, so my references are dated. In my time, Metal had already peaked as a scapegoat and the media had begun to focus on violent video games, a trend it's still riding as of this writing. *Mortal Kombat* was a big deal when it came out, because it was going to teach children how to rip each other's hearts out and *Doom* was going to teach us how to chop up a demon with a chainsaw. If you ask me, those are both useful skills. Plus, learning them took my mind off of my mucus for a while.

I likely think that whatever you do to make yourself feel better is stupid. And that's okay. You're not doing it to make me feel better, you're doing it for yourself. Plus, hating what you do makes me happy, so we all win.

It's tempting to write that you should never judge another person's coping mechanisms, but every time I think about that, the thought is immediately followed by "What about meth?" Meth might make some people feel better about life, but it does so by replacing their current problems with new problems such as "How can I get more of this ice?" and "How do I get these ants out of my skin?" Maybe we should never judge another person's coping mechanism as long as it's not causing that person more problems than they started with. As long as no one gets hurt, you know? Unless they want to get hurt. That's a grey area.

One of the uniting factors of the human race is that everyone big and small, rich and poor will have something shitty happen to them. Some of these things will be much shittier than others and some of these things will be problems with no solutions. I don't want to talk about the problems right now and I don't want to talk about the solutions. I want to talk about what people do when they're sick of dealing with the problems.

I very much wish that my coping mechanism involved swimming in a pool of money, Scrooge McDuck-style. It doesn't, both for health reasons and the fact that, depending on the denomination, I might have enough money to fill a large drinking glass. Instead, I listen to a lot of Iron Maiden. I imagine it's roughly the same feeling.

Music was always important to me. If you ask my mother, she will regale you with tales of me singing Huey Lewis songs around the house with a mic in my hand and the cord tucked into my diaper (maybe it's best that you don't ask her about that). However, it hit a turning point when I turned 11 and decided I was going to start playing the guitar that had been laying around the house since I was three. That act turned me into an active listener and gave music the foothold to take over my teenage years.

Prior to that, I played a lot of video games. I still play occasionally, though my consumption has dropped quite a bit since I stopped being cute enough for people to buy the games for me. However, they were very important to my early years, both as a way to pass the time and as a general interest. I spent a lot of my youth combing over video game magazines for the latest news and shakings from the industry. I didn't just want to play games, I wanted to know everything about them. I'm sure if the internet was widely available when I was younger, I would never have left the house.

These things can seem like a waste of time and sometimes that's all they are.

That's perfectly fine. Some people will tell you that you should never waste time, but they're wrong. There will come a point when you don't have time to waste and you'll have wished that you wasted it when you had it. These moments are often best wasted by just staring off into space, but sometimes you're not ready for that and you need something to stare at. It will help you in the long run, I promise.

As popular knowledge has it, sometimes shit happens. My grandfather died when I was 25. He was in his 80s, a lifelong smoker and had been in declining health for some years, so it was not an unexpected situation. However, we were very close, so I was little surprised when I didn't cry.

Now I'm not going to pretend that I'm some tremendous badass that never cries. Show me the first ten minutes of Pixar's *UP* and I can almost guarantee you that I will cry. Once, I watched that movie with the commentary on and still teared up. Fuck, when I was younger, I used to cry at the end of *Terminator 2*. If you catch me on the right day, I probably still will.

For a while, I felt guilty that I found the ending of *Terminator 2: Judgment Day* to be sadder than my grandfather's death. Since I could only cry at movies, I felt like some kind of monster. Movies are essentially flashing lights and sound. That's a stupid thing to cry about.

Movies are only flashing lights and sound, just like songs are a bunch of noises and books are a better organized alphabet soup. They don't require any more than a bit of your time and attention. When someone dies in a movie, you don't have to figure out who the executor of the estate is or make arrangements for a service or do anything but wait for the next flashing light to show up. It's a moment to reflect; a moment away from all the bullshit.

For most people, I think funerals are that moment. My grandfather didn't have a funeral; prior to his stroke, his instructions to me were to take him out in the woods and shoot him. He hated the idea of any sort of pageantry surrounding his death; he didn't even want an announcement in the paper. If I couldn't bring myself to shoot him, I suppose I had to honor at least some of his wishes. Plus, I've been to funerals and that's not the way I grieve. I'm not really sure how I grieve, but I know that's not it. Often the only way I know how to deal with things is to move forward.

This technique comes dangerously close to denial and I imagine that's a line that I've crossed before. Ignoring a problem is not dealing with it, but neither is dwelling on it. It's a tough balance. Going to the movies, listening to music, playing video games or reading a book is a way to take a moment and think without thinking. It's not quite being alone with your thoughts; it's like meeting your thoughts in a safe place with a mediator present to make sure you two don't kill each other. It was sad when Carl's wife died in *UP* or when the T-800 took that bath in the molten metal, but you only cry because it reminds you of other, sadder things that are a little closer to home. At least, that's what I think. Maybe I really am a monster.

If I am, I'm certainly a heathen one, because religion doesn't work for me. I tried. My mother was raised Catholic and continues to practice to this day. My father was not and does not. This created a schism when it came to me. It was eventually determined that I would be baptized into the church, but the decision to continue in the program was left to me, which is a nice way of saying that my Catholic career ended at baptism.

My mother made a valiant effort to get me to believe and for a while it worked. She bought me a *Reader's Digest Bible* that I still have to this day, because it's filled with awesome artwork and served as a great resource when I had to figure out what the hell these Metal bands were talking about (as anti-religious as the genre can be, a lot of lyrics are ripped right from the bible, though often inverted).

I don't remember the breaking point between believer and heathen, but it probably had to do with the seventh grade science teacher who taught evolution under duress. He made it very clear before we began that evolution was only a theory and he felt that theory had some serious holes in it. His preferred theory was covered in the *Book of Genesis*. The Board of Education did not consider the *Book of Genesis* a Science book, so he had to teach us evolution, though he snuck in some commentary about how ridiculous it was. Every time he showed us the remains of some proto-human, he'd say "But where's the missing link?" and the smiles of my classmates would beam in agreement (I don't know that every smile beamed in agreement, but some of them definitely did. Those are the ones I remember). That's when my innate sense of distrust kicked in. Outwardly, this appears to manifest itself as a strong curiosity, but that curiosity is driven by the feeling that someone is either lying to me or trying to keep something from me. I know that this sounds like paranoia and it very well may be, but I've managed to turn it into a healthy appetite for knowledge.

Which brings us back to the Bible. I was fine with it when I was younger, but the more I started to understand it and think into it, and the more I looked into the unabridged text, the less it started to resonate with me.

I'm not on board with a literal interpretation of the Bible, but even as a collection of stories, it doesn't hit me. I like the pictures though.

People will try to tell you how to cope and sometimes they'll force you to try their way, so the best advice I can give you is this: fuck 'em. It's your life and you can deal with it however you want. Some people will understand and some people will not. If your way of making sense of the world has anything to do with the word "sacred", I probably don't understand. That's okay, I don't have to. You may not understand Iron Maiden, heavy metal, horror movies, Swamp Thing or those bottles of honey that look like a bear, but you don't have to. Surely, if you don't, my heart breaks for you, but it doesn't affect my enjoyment. However, if you have a minute, I'd love to talk to you about what you're missing.

~~~~~

Solitary Refinement

The words "you don't understand" have long past the point of cliché. Every teenager has thought them, said them and then made fun of someone else for saying them. It's ironic, because the words are often spoken to people who either do understand and are trying to help or did understand and simply forgot. What makes it worse is that half the time you don't even understand yourself, but it feels easier to blame everyone else.

This feeling goes away usually, right around the time that the connections in your frontal lobe start functioning at an adult level. Echoes remain, as they always do in the wake of a tragic experience like being a teenager, which at least *feels* like a tragic experience to most, even if that seems ridiculous from the outside. A certain isolation is inherent there too, as you're just learning to connect and you barely know yourself.

I'm rambling on about teenagers because it's the closest parallel I can come up with for the isolation of disease. Your body changes in ways that make you feel different and it seems like no one understands. Often, they don't, because there's no way they can understand what it feels like. Sometimes it just seems that way.

I think I've met, in person, two people with Cystic Fibrosis. They were both in waiting rooms, though I'm only sure of the diagnosis on one of them. One was a lady who heard me cough and thought that I might have something to prevent her blood sugar from dropping. I never asked if she had CF and she never asked if I had Cystic Fibrosis Related Diabetes which, at the time, I didn't.

The other person was a nurse who my mom starting talking to about the wait in the Pulmonary Function Testing lab. Turns out the nurse was there to take the test too. It was nice, at the tender age of 8, to see someone who was 27 (my mom asked), had CF and wasn't dead.

Around that time, there were still CF summer camps where one could meet other kids with CF. Sounds like a great idea, right? It's a great way to show kids that they're not alone and that CF doesn't have to limit them. Of course, I was not the type of child who cared for the outdoors, socialization or places where you had to spend your summer waking up before noon, so I never attended, but I recognized the value inherent in them. Unfortunately, so did bacteria.

Bacteria love thick, delicious CF mucous because the viscosity gives them a chance to hang out and enjoy themselves. And since CF lungs are like special little snowflakes filled with cough scum, there's a CF lung for almost every type of bacteria.

Just wandering through the world, you're bound to find a type of bacteria that really likes what your lungs have to offer. You can get off to a decent start of a lifetime of infections and flare ups just by going through your everyday motions, but sometimes you get sick of growing the same bacteria again and again. If you really want to try something new, you need to trade with your friends.

Bacteria figured this out before we did. You put a bunch of people with CF in a room and you have a bunch of lungs growing a bunch of different bacteria. Why not share? Bacteria will turn any gathering of CF patients into a key party where everyone leaves with a different lung. As you can imagine, this is a problem. The camps had to go.

Now there are infection guides in place and CF patients are encouraged to keep a safe distance from each other. A lot of people believe they shouldn't even be in the same room together, even if contact is limited and a mask is worn.

The risk of infection with CF slowly teaches you how to exclude yourself from things. It can also make a handy excuse to get out of things you didn't feel like doing, particularly in the winter when everyone is sick and you shouldn't be anywhere near them. That's a classic example of lemons into lemonade.

It's much easier to think everyone knows what's happening with you than to actually explain it. This is what makes screaming "You don't understand!" look like a good idea. Often, the reason people don't understand is because you didn't tell them.

What makes it hard is that you develop a shorthand with your disease and it shuts people out. For example, when I say I need to take my pills, I mean my enzymes. If I need to refer to other pills, I will call them by name. My pills are my enzymes or, as I should probably refer to them, my digestive enzymes. I can't even define it without leaving something out.

Just think about giving someone directions to your house and how much you have to think that through. You come home pretty much every day, but turning that action into words to make someone else understand that process can be hard because you don't even think about it anymore. You've internalized the process, which increases the potential for miscommunication and frustration.

The fact that you have two reference points helps; you know where they're starting from and you know where you want them to end. You can also draw on some of your overlapping personal experience to build a shared shorthand (instead of saying "drive 2.3 miles and bear left", you can say "bear left at the old shanty town"). And if all else fails, they can just look it up on the internet.

Directions have a definite outcome and you can judge their effectiveness by whether or not the person got to your house in a timely manner. This book is filled with strange metaphors because it's often the only way I know how to communicate some of my internal processes. I don't know how to describe my mucus to someone who's not already familiar with it and I'm not sure how to tell you what it feels like when my lungs are filled with it. We're missing the reference points, because I don't know your experience and you don't know mine. It's a struggle both to explain and to understand. Think about how often this happens in our everyday lives. Think about how often we just abort communications when it becomes too much of a struggle. I'm guilty of it a lot, both as a talker and a listener. I am notoriously impatient with people who don't understand technology and I will often just fix their problem instead of showing them how to fix their problem. There's not enough common ground there for me to feel like I'm saying anything that's going to help them. It saddens me to think how often I might do that when someone has an actual problem, not just a broken laptop.

The answer to this problem is questions. Ask questions. Don't ask with any agenda other than to start a conversation. Just ask a question. If a person wants to answer it, they will. If they do, all you have to do is listen. If not, try asking another one. If they tell you to fuck off, then fuck off for a while. You can come back and try again later. I think it's really important to give people an opening where they can just drop a bunch of information on you. Maybe they want to talk to you about a book they read or maybe they want to talk about their divorce. Maybe they'll ask you a question because they just want to hear someone else talk for a while. Maybe, and this might sound a little out there, they are genuinely curious about what is happening in your life. If they are, don't hesitate to tell them, even if you're not sure how. Perhaps you'll eventually build some common ground.

Sometimes writing this book was simply a matter of sitting down at the computer and letting the words happen. Other times, I came close to drilling a hole in my head to see if I could trepan some of the words out. I went years without trying to communicate this stuff to anyone. I could never find the words. I'm not sure that my family—save for my mother, who took me to my appointments for 18 years—knows a lot of this stuff. I'm not sure anyone needs to know this stuff. Either way, I'm writing it down.

~~~~~~

Total Cost of Ownership

Total cost of ownership, or TCO, takes into account all the money you will spend in order to purchase and use a product or system. For example, the TCO of a house involves everything from electricity and water to taxes and maintenance. Even if the initial cost of ownership is low, that house is useless without electricity and roof repairs. You may have inherited the house, but you still have to make sure you can afford it.

I did not inherit a house. I inherited a van once, but the TCO on that mostly involved towing it to the junkyard. I also inherited Cystic Fibrosis. Had I known the TCO on that, I probably would have refused it, but I thought I could handle it at the time. Not that what I thought mattered.

Luckily, when I was younger, my parents floated most of the expenses for me. Without them, I don't know what I would have done. There just weren't a lot of job opportunities for a 3 year old back then. It's not like it is today. There seemed to be a fair amount of interest in the *Ghostbusters 2* spec script I'd been working on and I could sing a mean version of "The Heart of Rock and Roll", but I was having trouble monetizing these skills in a meaningful manner.

At age 5, I made the tough decision to go to school full time. Again, it was a competitive job market and I needed every advantage I could get. Plus, going to school let me stay on my parent's insurance, which was a great help at a time when I really needed it.

Apparently I was a slow learner, because I didn't finish school until I was 18. I had a few jobs during that time, but nothing that could really make a dent in the cost of CF. So, I took some classes at a community college in hopes of getting a better position in the tough job market. At least that's what I told everyone. Really, I didn't care what I went for, I was just looking to sponge off of my parent's insurance for a couple more years. I figured I'd show up, bang out a couple of classes, get a degree in an up and coming field and watch the checks start to pile up.

I signed up as a Photonics major, because I heard it involved lasers and from what I learned from the documentary *Terminator 2: Judgment Day*, lasers were going to be very important in the future. It turns out that an Associate's Degree from a community college doesn't put you on a fast track to your very own T-800. I'm pretty good at school, but I don't care for it at all, so I find it all too tempting to show up, get the grades and get out without learning a goddamn thing. Say what you will about the low level third shift hotel job I had at the time, but it got me closer to building a terminator than college did, partly because they paid me and partly because nothing happens at night, so there's plenty of time for outside projects (okay, I never came close to building a terminator, but if you have a broken Sega Dreamcast, I can probably fix it).

The law at the time made it so that if I was in school, I'd have access to my parent's insurance until I was 21, but in trying to turn a two year degree into three years of insurance, I fell short by one semester. So, I did the only logical thing: I signed up and paid for an extra semester of school that I never attended. I could have gone to a 4 year university and stayed on the insurance until I was 25, but the idea of that made me sicker, so I couldn't go through with it. Plus, I was working full time at the hotel, so I should have been all set.

Unfortunately, I had a bit of a drug problem. After taxes, I was pulling down about $300 a week at the hotel, which felt like decent money to a kid fresh out of community college, but it wasn't quite enough to put a dent in the $6000 worth of drugs I was using every month. So, as the story so often goes, I ended up at the Department of Social Services, looking for a little state assistance to ease the burden of my drug use.

Now, I know that some of you are probably thinking that I was an entitled welfare queen, but let me assure you, the state social worker was way ahead of you on that. Though I carry some physical signs of Cystic Fibrosis—clubbed fingers, barrel chest and, at the time, very low weight—to the untrained eye, I just look like an alcoholic. So, the social worker wasn't completely out of line when he asked "Why are you here?" As I was pleading my case ("C'mon man, just one fix!"), he saw that I had a discount card for a local music store in my wallet. This lead him to the idea that my best option would be to "reform the rock group Creed". I could think of at least 4 reasons why that wouldn't work, but kept them to myself because I really wanted that insurance. After a tense negotiation, he said that I would be eligible for state insurance if I could show $600 in medical expenses. This was small medical potatoes to me, so I easily came up with a $600 bill and went on my way. I was set for life!

"Life" in this case refers to a measurement of time equivalent to 6 months, as my eligibility went up for review twice a year. If I got a pay raise or a new job, I had to show more medical expenses and the amount I had to show kept climbing and climbing. It wasn't easy. I had quite a few lapses in coverage. I once charged a $1900 prescription to my credit card just to get a hit (by "just to get a hit" I mean "because I was trying so hard to move mucus that I had started coughing up blood"). I tried to live poor just to keep the insurance coming, but I have expensive tastes. Cinnamon Toast Crunch doesn't buy itself.

I'm sure that somewhere there are 18 year olds who have their shit together and their life mapped out. I was not one of them. I wasn't so sure I'd have much of a life past 18, so I didn't spend a lot of time thinking about a future that did not involve sending a naked Arnold Schwarzenegger cyborg back in time to kill John Connor. I will admit that I did not handle the transition to adulthood well. But, in my defense, the transition is not easy. I'm approaching 30 now and I still haven't completely stuck the landing. Why didn't I just get a job with insurance? I was young. I felt like it was enough just to have a job. Plus, even if you have a job with insurance, there's a solid chance that my CF thinks your prescription plan is fucking stupid. My mom worked for almost 30 years at a popular drug store chain that had decent coverage for doctor's visits, but a prescription plan that wouldn't piss on my lungs if they were on fire. And let's not forget the time there was a problem with my father's insurance plan and they sent us a bill for $20,000. It's not easy. It takes practice. Plus, you never know if you're going to wake up one day and feel like someone is trying to use your lungs as a Jell-O mold. So

I had to find a job with insurance that I could still do at a semi-competent level even if I felt like shit. I eventually managed, but it certainly wasn't a graceful and intuitive journey.

It also took a while to break me of the notion that I could do whatever I wanted. By that, I don't mean that I expected to sit around the house, buck naked and shitting on a newspaper I laid on floor; I just mean it took me a long time to accept that CF limited my options. Though I've had it for my entire life, it never made major decisions for me. It gave me a lot more to do in order to keep myself in top shape and it required me to make a lot of little adjustments in my day to day life, but this was the first time I actually felt like it was limiting me. As I learned from that time I put on "You Could Be Mine" by Guns 'n Roses and stripped the skin off my hand, I do not have a T-800 endoskeleton: I am not a robot. And neither are you. Nor are most of the people you meet (the jury is still out on a few of them). It is ridiculous and ineffective to pretend otherwise. I should have prepared myself better, but I was young and I felt like I had a chance of not having to deal with it. But statistics don't get diseases, people do. And it's easy to forget that while something like CF will definitely fuck up your body, it can also fuck up your mind.

For those of you who have a disease, I wish I had an easy solution for you. I ended up finding a job in a call center that allowed me to spend most of my time sitting on my ass and kept me away from handling a lot of money and germs and stuff, so that worked well. If you're having trouble finding insurance, there's a chance you might be eligible for an assistance program run by the manufacturers of your medications. There's also a number of assistance programs for hospital care and doctor visits. The internet is your friend. And don't be afraid to ask someone for help. You may end up doing a lot of searching before you find what you need, but help will be out there somewhere. And if you need to use some kind of government assistance program, people may judge you, but it's better for them to judge you while you're alive than celebrate your stoic commitment to social mores in death.

~~~~~

Stabbing the Antichrist

There are days when I feel impossibly run down. On those days, I can't point to any one thing that's wrong with me, but I feel the need to sleep the day away and recharge myself. I'm perfectly happy to sleep all that time, so it's not depression. I think I just spend so much time making my body do things it doesn't feel like doing that sometimes it says "Fuck you" and shuts down for a while.

This is a roundabout way of saying that occasionally my fiancee thinks she's going to enjoy an evening of witty repartee, but instead ends up enjoying some Netflix and the sound of my sleep farts. For her, it's probably just as exciting as it sounds, but I assure you that I'm having a goddamn blast.

On one such evening, Bekka decided to watch *The Omen* (The good one. She's not a monster). I was fading in and out of consciousness while it was on, but I've seen it so many times that my body instinctively knows to wake up when someone is about to die. My body has failed me a lot in life, but times like that make up for it.

The Omen is the touching story of a woman who gives birth to a child that dies about an hour later. Her husband, wanting to shield his beloved wife from the misery of the situation, gives some nuns the go ahead to replace their dead baby with the offspring of a mother who died in childbirth. What the nuns do not mention is that the mother was a jackal and the child is the antichrist. Love conquers all, right?

Love doesn't conquer much in *The Omen*, but the child does. Throughout the movie, Damien uses his diabolical influence to make some terrible things happen, such as nanny suicide and photographer decapitation. His adopted father is told how to stop this, but it would mean stabbing the child he's raised as his son. There's some back and forth as to whether or not he can do that, but he eventually decides to take up the seven daggers required and have a go at it. As he's about to do the deed on a church altar, Damien looks up with his cherubic young face and says "No Daddy, please" or something like that. His father hesitates and pays the price by dying. Spoiler alert, the movie ends with Damien gloating over the caskets of his dead adoptive parents. It's fucking awesome.

Bekka has a child, and a wonderful child at that, so upon viewing the final confrontation between Gregory Peck and the 5 year old Antichrist, she remarked that she would never be able to finish the job; motherhood has blessed her with empathy and a sense of protection. Even though Damien was adopted and probably the antichrist, she would not be able to end his life. Perhaps, as in *Rosemary's Baby*, she could use her love to try and redeem the child.

I do not have children. I can't have children. The tube that leads the sperm from their testicular habitat does not exist in my sack. Anything that comes out is all show. So, if we somehow end up as caretakers for the Antichrist, I will have no problems stabbing him.

Not that I believe in the Antichrist —or even the regular Christ for that matter—this is just a hypothetical situation. Then again, maybe the fact that I can't reproduce is proof of a higher power.

I was 18 when my mother first floated the idea that 99% of male Cystic Fibrosis patients are infertile. I'm not sure why it came up on the ride home from one of my regular checkups, but it may have had something to do with the fact that I had just received a book on CF and I was about to find out anyway. Maybe she didn't want me to storm down the stairs and scream "WHY DID YOU KEEP THIS FROM ME! I'LL NEVER SIRE AN HEIR!!" I wouldn't have. When she told me, I just pretended I knew anyway. I did not.

I don't know that I ever planned on having children, but it's one thing to decide you aren't going to do something and another thing to be told that you can't do something. Normally, when told I can't do something, I go out of my way to do it. I did not go out of my way to have children, so I suppose there's your answer right there.

As I mentioned before, people with CF are not sterile due to lack of sperm, but they often lack the equipment needed to lead the sperm out of the testicles. Some CF mutations manifest a blockage in the vas deferens that keeps the sperm from coming out, but my mutation (homogenous delta-F508) often prevents the actual formation of the vas deferens. Everything else works fine, but that tube is missing. If I believed in things, I'd say it was the universe's subtle hint that it didn't want more of me. Luckily, I don't believe in things.

For years, that piece of trivia was the entirety of what I knew about my situation, because it really didn't matter. Through careful planning and general misanthropy, I avoided the type of situations that would lead to questions of fertility. Eventually, once I decided to stop living like a crazy cat lady who didn't care for pets, Bekka got a little curious about my fertility situation and whether or not she needed the IUD she'd been carrying around in her uterus. And that's how I ended up having my ballsack kneaded like bread dough while she watched.

It did not happen like that right away. At first, there was some hope that the doctors would be able to spot my vas deferens (or lack of one) through a testicular ultrasound I had. Unfortunately, my majestic testicles blocked any clear view of the surrounding area. At least, that's what I'm told. I've asked for copies of the pictures, but every time I bring it up, everyone seems to think I'm joking. Probably because I start laughing when I think about writing "It's a boy!" on them and hanging them on the refrigerator.

The most accurate way to check fertility is to have a semen analysis, but that would have required my insurance to pay for it, which they wouldn't. And given that I don't have money to just throw away by going to a lab to do the thing I do at home when I don't have any money to do anything else, I wouldn't pay for it either.

My stubborn refusal to pay to jack off led to another option: having a doctor feel around for a vas deferens.

One of my regular CF doctors referred me to a urologist at the same hospital who was willing to feel around my nutsack for sign of a sperm delivery system. Not wanting to be the only one in the room who had already seen my balls, I brought Bekka along.

When we were called into the room, we were greeted by a nice young lady who was one of the fellows in the urology department. She asked a few questions and then I laid on a table and took my balls out. She felt around for a while and thought there might be some kind of vas deferens on the right testicle, which I found slightly frightening, but she couldn't be sure, so she called in the head of the department to cop a feel.

This is the part where two people kneaded my balls like bread dough.

Technically, Bekka did not get to see that part, as I was behind a curtain at the time, but she did see two doctors working very hard on something. What they were working on was searching my ball sack for a piece of spaghetti protruding from each nut. They didn't find anything of note.

When one is kicked in the balls, the pain is immediate and intense. It hurts from your balls all the way into your stomach and you instinctively double over in pain. The pain of having your balls kneaded is different. It's a slow ache, a gradual realization of "I don't like the turn this has taken." It certainly didn't rank up with the worst pain I've felt, but I would say I'd go out of my way to keep it from happening again.

All told, my balls were kneaded for about 10 minutes. Afterward, the head of the department drew an impressively detailed diagram of the average testicle on the back of a business card and told me about the spaghetti thing. He said that he didn't feel a convincing vas in either side, but the only way to be sure was to perform a semen analysis. And with that, I agreed to pay someone to let me jack off in a hospital.

I did not, however, go through with it. I had scheduled a follow up appointment with the urologist, but given that my insurance wouldn't pay for that or the test, I ended up canceling. Plus, this was in the winter and there was a lot of snow that year, which makes it hard to both get to the hospital and to keep from jacking off for the requisite 3 days required by the test. To make up for it, every once in a while, I just feel around and make sure no tubes have magically sprouted.

We did not go through all of this to have children; we wanted to make sure I couldn't have children. I don't think I should anyway. I know that some people with CF have had sperm removed in order to have a family, but I have to assume they are more well adjusted than me. I spend so much time thinking about my health and taking care of myself that it feels almost unfair for me to bring a dependent into the world. Plus, if Bekka and I are somehow tasked with defeating a 5 year old antichrist, someone has to be able to do the deed.

~~~~~~

The Incredible Mucus Filled Boy

Having a disease is a perfect supervillain origin moment, but luckily illness can also keep someone in check. There could be an entire population of supervillains in waiting who are just too damn tired to enact their terrible scheme. Maybe CF is the Superman to my Lex Luthor, thwarting my plans and holding me back from taking over the world.

Not everyone who is sick is a supervillain waiting to happen, just like not everyone who is sick is a courageous angel. The thing about diseases is that all kinds of people get them, the key word being "people." Human beings can be fucked up, selfish, kind, loving, petty, jealous, sincere, assholes, generous, neurotic and polite, sometimes within the course of a single day. Having a disease does not absolve anyone of these qualities. Their life does not consist of slow motion footage of them weakly smiling in a hospital while a piano ballad plays in the background. They do not simply become a disease.

Would I feel the same way if we traded the stirring piano ballads for 10 foot tall banners of the Incredible Mucus Filled Boy? No, I absolutely wouldn't. But that's because I'm under no pressure to turn into a carnival sideshow, both because the sideshow barely exists anymore and Cystic Fibrosis is not a very visual disease. And while having people pay to stare at you sounds like a dream job to me, I'm sure there's a downside I'm discounting. But it'd be nice to take a break from being a courageous angel.

That's a lot to live up to. When I was in my late-teens/early twenties, the idea was always in the back of my head that if people really knew me, they wouldn't want me cured. I'm not a very sympathetic person. If you laid a piano ballad over slow motion footage of me going to check the mail or making a sock puppet or something, you'd probably expect narration detailing the day I snapped. It's a long road from there to courageous angel. And there's a lot of pressure to get there.

The strangest manifestation of this pressure is that at 22 years old, I attempted to write a book about Cystic Fibrosis. The thesis of that book was that sometimes bad things happen to bad people (such as myself) and that you should actually feel good about that. I only finished two chapters, now lost due to poor data backup habits, but I assure you that they were hilarious.

That book, though unfinished, was very important. Up to that point, I spent years training my brain to not think of myself as someone with Cystic Fibrosis. Doing so is equivalent to climbing the roof thinking you're Superman and then being surprised when the day ends with both your legs broken and massive head trauma. Pretending you are something you are not will not make it true. Going full speed at a roadblock doesn't make it disappear. You have to drive around it.

I was scared of the part of my brain that amends all of my accomplishments with "…for someone with a lung disease" or some variation thereof. "Oh wow, that was a great workout…for someone with a lung disease." "I'm sure you'd be more successful professionally if you didn't have a lung disease." "You look great today…for someone with a lung disease." I figured I could silence it by just pretending I wasn't any different from anyone else.

I failed to silence that voice. I also failed to silence the cough that shot mucus out of my mouth on a daily basis.

Learning to ignore was useless for me; learning to adjust was key. Adaptability was and is very important. The world will keep turning no matter how much lung butter I'm churning.

I hate being told what to do, especially by my own body. Sometimes I get sick of finding the little roads and pathways around CF and I just run straight at the brickwall like it isn't even there. I always regret it. Not immediately, but these things catch up to you. I can no longer take the train into the city, walk 8 blocks to and from a 3 hour concert and expect to be bright and cheerful the next day. It takes me at least a week to recover.

But that could just as easily be an age thing. My real fear is that CF really isn't holding me back at all.

I'm terrified that I might be lazy. As it stands, I do a lot of laying down and I always make room for a nap. I sincerely hope this is because I have a lung disease, otherwise all the procrastination, laziness and malaise was me the whole time.

This is why I'm scared of a cure. Ridiculous, right? Well, I'm certainly not scared in the way that would keep me from taking whatever cure they cook up. It's more akin to the fear one has when starting a new job or meeting someone new. It's almost like stage fright. Like I'd finally be stepping up to the big time and we're going to find out if I have what it takes or if I should have never left my small, mucus-filled pond.

I sometimes like to think about how I would have turned out if I didn't have CF, but the concept is completely alien to me. I wonder how much of what little I've accomplished has been the result of the drive I get from the feeling of having one metaphorical hand tied behind my back. Without CF, would I just find another place to get that? Divorce, maybe? Or, would my parents have stayed together if all this child rearing was just a little easier? I know that sounds like a dark line of thinking, but it's an interesting thought.

For the record, I think the early part of my life would have been very similar, because I was somewhat oblivious to the idea that I was different anyway. Perhaps my parents would have held on a little longer, but that union was always doomed to failure. I probably would have moved to the big city at a young age, working menial go-nowhere jobs to support my burgeoning music/writing career while taking classes in some form of science. Probably neuro. I then would have had a mental breakdown and ran back to whatever home would take me, while I restarted my life in a small town like some crappy 90s sitcom character.

Judging from my half-brother Jake, I would have probably broken 6 foot something if CF had not stunted my growth. Then again, he does have a different mother, so maybe that's where all the tall genes are. At the very least, maybe my wrists would not have roughly the same diameter as a large railroad spike.

Or I could be completely wrong.

If a cure showed up right now, I'd probably just amend that voice in my head to "...for someone who was born with a lung disease" or some other tripe. There's always an excuse. It's too late to find out what it would be like to not have CF at all; it has had enough years to do enough physical and mental damage that I will never completely be rid of it. Thinking about what kind of person I would be if I never had CF will never be anything more than that: a though. But, as much as it scares me, I'm ready to find out what it would be like to be cured.

~~~~~~

The Act of Creation

If failure has become a constant theme in this book, I assure you that it's only because failure is a constant theme in my life. I am of the opinion that failure should be a constant theme in most lives, so I encourage you to go fail at something right now. It could be anything: long division, marathon running, bowel control, the list goes on. I'm not saying you should try to fail, but you should try pouring your entire heart into something you're not sure you can accomplish. Most actions have a desired outcome, but even when that goal is not reached, the process is important.

One of my favorite things to do is make stuff. If left alone for a long enough period, I will eventually try to create something. I don't even particularly care what it is. A lot of it, seemingly, has no value. When I was younger, I used to make stop motion movies. The only time anyone ever saw them was when my Mom would inquire about how the family video camera became Jay's video camera. The answer, of course, was through a series of Joker vs. Godzilla stop motion films.

These shorts weren't great or even good, which is why I didn't show them to anyone. They were just fun to make. It was about seeing if I could tell a story with a couple of cheap toys and a free afternoon.

That's a perfectly acceptable thing for a kid to do, right?

Probably, but I was 14.

I was possibly the only 14 year old who purchased a *Batman and Robin* playset because I felt like it would bring my productions to the next level. I would love to pretend to be embarrassed by this, but I'm not. Had we gotten a camera earlier, it's extremely possible that I would have ended up as the goddamn king of stop motion. Or not. Maybe I would have just had a few more years of fun and learned something in the process. Would any of that knowledge be of any use in the real world? Who knows? More importantly, who cares?

I made those movies for about two years. The circumstances were not conducive to stop motion. Our apartment was small, so it wasn't like I could leave a bunch of toys hanging around for days at a time. I persevered for a while, but once I got a four track, the game was over.

Since this is a mostly digital world now, I feel like I have to explain what a four track is. A four track takes a standard audio cassette and allows you to layer four separate recordings on it and play them back at the same time. This was fucking amazing to me. Sure, I had been aware of multitrack technology for some time, but to have it in my own home was mind blowing. I could record one guitar, go back, record a second guitar, add some vocals and slap an entertainment center to mimic some drums. There were times that I got so excited about it that I just ran around the house. If I think about it really hard, I still kind of want to.

Like pretty much everyone ever, I play guitar. I started when I was around 11 years old. I took lessons for about a year, but did a lot of my learning just through playing other people's songs. Being that I'm not a joiner of things, I never wanted to join a band or anything. I just wanted to make songs. Before I had my four track, recording these songs relied on the incredible patience (and eight track!) of our school's music teacher. Make no mistake; these songs were fucking terrible. How Mr. B sat through any of those grueling "performances" is completely beyond me. Some deep part of my brain knew they sucked at the time, but there was a limited window in which I could record and I would be goddamned if I didn't make something. As the type of guy who has a lot of shitty ideas before I stumble on something usable, this arrangement wasn't conducive to my musical growth. Having my own four track meant that every stolen riff and terrible lyric could be saved analyzed and destroyed on my own time. It was fantastic.

At home, I could pull the type of weird shit that no one but me should ever have to sit through. I once used my four track, in conjunction with my home stereo, to make an 8 part harmony. I wanted to make a joke here about how I wasted my teenage years, but I can't. I was having a blast!

My friend Anthony eventually played drums on two albums worth of songs I had written. Almost without exception, they were terrible. His performance was great; my ability to produce a recording was questionable and my song writing skills were almost non-existent. It was mostly riffs I stole from KISS and Alice Cooper. I also tried to re-write Guns n' Roses' "You Could Be Mine" at least three times. It never went well.

My senior year of high school, things changed. My mother finally bought a home computer and I took my first bold step into digital production. Using a copy of Pro Tools Free and the internal soundcard, I turned the family computer into an ersatz digital 8 track. I used this technology to make some terrible noises. I used a computer mic to record my guitar, giving it roughly the same presence it would have if my amp was a cordless phone and the drum program I used produced sounds roughly equivalent to those old Hit Stix toys from the 80s. It may have actually been a step back from the four track.

However, I did not let that deter me. I kept making albums, writing songs and learning about recording for years. I, along with my friends Andy and Tom, even did some live performances. I bought my own computer, added some equipment, read some magazines, took some equipment away and eventually made some things I'm actually proud of. Those things would not exist if I didn't spend all those years making complete shit. The process is important. Even if, before I started, I knew that my best selling recording would top out around 58 albums, I still would have made it. After a while, I just posted them all for free on the internet anyway (though I do accept donations; I'm not here to refuse money).

Why was the process so important? What did I learn? Well, I learned a lot about computers and how audio worked. I learned a fair amount of music theory. I can do minor guitar repairs. I learned some synthesis. But I also learned a lot about myself. I know that sounds totally clichéd and stupid, but it's true. For years, if I wanted to know what I thought about something, I wrote a song about it. I got a lot of things out that way. I also learned how to tackle projects, create goals and, possibly more importantly, how to walk away and cool off for a while. Could I have learned all of this some other way? Sure, there are tons of ways to learn things. But these are things that cannot be told to you. That's why the process is important.

In the summer of 2011, I had been taking care of my grandmother, but it started to become clear that she needed more attention than I could provide. Since our financial situation wouldn't provide for any home care services, we decided to move closer to my father and stepmother so they could help out with her. We signed the lease on a two bedroom apartment and I started moving everything in (this process wasn't so important; moving is always terrible). Unfortunately, somewhere in this time frame Gram fell down and broke her hip. This meant she was going to need even more care than originally assumed, so she ended up staying full time at my father's house for a few months. Given that we had already signed the lease on the apartment and moved all the stuff in, I stayed there for a little while, but I wasn't able to afford it on my own. Gram was able to help out for a little while, but once her dementia took over, she decided that she hated living at my father's house. Things got really ugly. I felt terrible because she really wanted to come live with me, but there was no way I could make that happen. She needed 24 hour care, so we ended up putting her in a home, which I still feel terrible about. She seems to like it quite a bit though. It's a good place for her to be, because it's filled with people for her to talk to. Though she'll tell you she doesn't like having all those people around, she's lying.

The only thing she loves more than having all those visitors is complaining about having all those visitors. She's done it her entire life.

I'm kind of glossing over this stuff, because this was a terrible time and it's still a little too recent for me to write about it with any kind of clarity. The point is, I ended up with a bedroom I didn't need and an apartment I couldn't afford, so I had to break the lease. Since trying to float that apartment for a couple of months had destroyed my savings, I ended up moving into my father's house. Not wanting to be an imposition to anyone, I tend to stay to one room of the house. Really, we all kind of do. Plus, my stepmother smokes and though she only does it in her room, it's probably best for me to stay close to my air filter. But, given that my room isn't huge, I don't have enough room to lay out all my recording equipment. It's been about a year since I've recorded any new music. I suppose that's how I started writing this book. All that energy had to go somewhere.

In writing this book, I wrote a lot of words that won't ever see the light of day. That may seem like a waste of time, but had I not written those words, I never would have gotten to the ones that made it into the book. The process is important. I encourage everyone reading this to write a book. It doesn't even need to be a book about yourself; you can write anything. It's fascinating. I've learned a lot about myself and how I feel about CF and the rest of my life. Even if no one else ever reads this, it will have been worth it.

But you should still tell all your friends to read it.

~~~~~

Appendix: Diabetes Food Diary

In writing about major life events, the minutia often gets lost. This is necessary for a compelling narrative, but does a disservice to how hard it is to adjust to change. What follows is not a compelling narrative; it's all the minutia.

Sometime in 2008, I was diagnosed with Cystic Fibrosis Related Diabetes or CFRD. I was not happy about it. I could live with not being able to breathe; not being able to enjoy a soda seemed like a death sentence to me. Of course, it wasn't, but I also don't want to sell the idea that I gracefully made the transition overnight. It was a long awkward process to find out what my diet was going to be.

Given my body's absolute refusal to gain weight, a diet of salad and turnips, though great for my blood sugar levels, was never going to work for me. When I was first diagnosed with CFRD, I tipped the scales at 130 pounds. Being that I'm just over 5'9", that's not quite enough pounds to keep me from looking like an amazing feat of lifelike puppetry. To fix that my diet needs to take into account my body's inability to handle sugar with my body's inability to efficiently digest food.

Thankfully, I have pills that both help me process sugar and digest my damn food. Since I've been taking the digestive pills for as long as I can remember, I know how they work. You will not see them mentioned in the following diary, but I assure you that I took them.

You will, however, see me mention Prandin. Prandin is a tiny pill that tells my pancreas to push out some more insulin to deal with all the incoming glucose. I was instructed that I should never take more than 4 with a meal and encouraged by my doctors to keep a diary of my meals and blood sugar. Given the state of my pancreas, it was questionable as to whether or not Prandin would even work for me, so the diary was to answer that question and help me parse out what my exact dosage would be, as it changes depending on the carb content of whatever I ate. Very simply, more carbohydrates=more pills.

Somewhat more complex is the fact that different kinds of carbs affect blood sugar differently. Complex carbohydrates, such as those in wheat bread, take longer to enter the blood stream than something like a spoonful of sugar. Meals with high fat content can also delay the absorption of glucose in the blood.

There are other factors that can affect blood sugar as well, such as sleep, exercise, health and stress level, but you'll rarely find those mentioned in the following pages. In fact, you won't find the fat content, carb content or really any details about the meals

I ate, save for what I ate and if I enjoyed it. I believe I meant to look all that up later. I never did.

In that respect, this diary is kind of half assed, but it's fun to see how slow the process of change was for me. There was a short period where I cut carbs completely and I like to remember myself like that—the type of person who can adjust to change at a moment's notice. I am not. Reading back through this diary, I'm shocked at how much regular soda I was drinking. I would never try that now, because regular soda is filled with empty calories that drop glucose in my blood way too fast. Though I pretty much gave the finger to everyone who said you could get used to diet soda, they were right. And at this point, I don't even drink much diet soda; I drink mostly water (but don't let me bullshit you, if it's summer, you'll probably find me with a Polar Diet Orange Dry in my hand).

You'll also notice that I'm eating a bizarre amount of food at 4 in the morning. That's because at the time this diary was written, I was working third shift in a casino call center and we got one free meal in the cafeteria. I always tried to make the most of that meal. Plus, I was trying really hard to gain weight (for the record, the Prandin help me put on about 10 pounds, but my weight gain didn't really take off until I started a daily proton pump inhibitor that kept my stomach acid from tearing up the pills I took for digestion).

As for the writing the diary, being that this was before I had a phone that could tell me the carb content of my meal and take a picture of it to show my friends, I was carrying around a notebook and filling it with my serial killer hand writing (actually, I imagine serial killers have meticulous hand writing. I guess I just like the term). I've typed it all out here so that you don't have to waste time going "Is that an 'a' or an '8'", but I've kept to the original form as much as possible, while adding notes for clarity and occasionally fixing the spelling. There's a lot in here that borders on product placement (and even a couple foods that have been discontinued), but it was in the original, so I've carried it over. Also, I'm not sure if the plural form of Prandin is "Prandin" or "Prandins", but I seemed to have been under the impression that it was the former, so I stuck with it.

As the units, blood sugar is measured in milligrams per deciliter or mg/dl. You stab yourself with a lancet—usually on the finger, though at the time I was using my palm—draw some blood, put it on a test strip and your glucose meter will tell you how much sugar you have coursing through your body.

I try to keep my fasting blood sugars around 100 mg/dl and my post-meal (roughly 2 and a half hours after eating) under 180 mg/dl, though at the time I considered anything under 200 to be a victory.

11/21/2008
12:00am
Attempting to drink Propel Fitwater. Woefully unimpressed. Hoping it's because I recently brushed my teeth. Pretty sure it's not.

This is America. We are supposed to be on the cutting edge and we can't make a low carb beverage that doesn't taste like getting punched in the mouth.

2:55am
Drank cup of Earl Grey with 2 packets of honey. Refuse to sacrifice taste for the subtle sense of sophistication this lends me.

3:33am
Pre-Meal Blood Sugar: 162 mg/dl
I ate 3 hot dogs and a pile of bacon. It was cafeteria food and henceforth not nearly as awesome as it sounds. I took 1 Prandin.

6:15am

Post-Meal Blood Sugar: 68 mg/dl
I felt a little faint. I think the pills work. Also a convenient excuse to drink some Dr. Pepper.

7:33pm
Pre-Meal Blood Sugar: 96 mg/dl
I had a Boost (high protein), a large roast beef grinder and a Diet Dr. Pepper. It really does taste more like regular Dr. Pepper. Except for the aftertaste. That tastes like ass. *(Note: According to the next entry, I only took 1 pill. That's some quality reporting on my part).*

10:30pm
Post-Meal: 198 mg/dl
Probably could have taken two pills, but I was a little gun shy after last night's debacle.

11/22/2008
4:00am
Pre-Meal: 102 mg/dl
I ate a monte cristo and a pile of French fries covered in cheese and bacon bits. I started off drinking water, but had a small sip of apple juice, because I'm pretty sure all these diet drinks are leading to severe depression.

I also took 2 Prandin because I work at a casino and it feeds my gambler's mentality. If I die, I will attempt to check this box before I drop *(Note: in this space I drew a box which remained unchecked)*.

6:35am
With one testing strip left I decided to mess up and apply the blood all half-assedly. We'll just have to guess the result. It feels around 190 or so.

8:30am
I ate a Snicker Energy Bar. My furnace was busted, so I was too cold and cranky to check my blood sugar. Wilfred Brimley would not be pleased. I took a Prandin and went to sleep.

8:05pm
Pre-Meal: 114 mg/dl
I had a large roast beef grinder and a diet A&W cream soda that was surprisingly delicious. I'm still not sold on the aftertaste, but as long as I never stop drinking, I'm fine.

10:35pm
Post-Meal: 163 mg/dl
Either the Prandin is working or I'm doing this wrong. This reading does come after a 10 minute bout of vigorous exercise. By "vigorous exercise" I mean I bought 2 new songs for *Rock Band 2* and I hit the drums like they owe me money. I'm about to enjoy a victory bowl of Campbell's

Roadhouse Chili along with 2 Prandin. I will then drive to work. If someone finds my corpse halfway through a tree, please fill in the estimated time of death here: _____. Thank you.

11/23/2008
1:28am
Post-Post Meal: 120 mg/dl
Figured I'd check up after the chili. Probably didn't need two Prandin for it, but I feel like I could punch out walrus right now.

3:15am
Pre-Meal: 100 mg/dl
Having had 2 rather successful Prandin adventures, I went all out with a bacon cheeseburger (with bun, which I normally discard), a pile of French fries (covered in A1) and some corned beef with mustard sauce. I attempted to wash it down with some Cran-Apple abomination that one is supposed to mix with water, but I'm still trying to choke that down as I write this. I hope whoever invented diet drinks is dead, because it saves me the trouble of killing them.

6:00am
Post-Meal: 125 mg/dl
Somehow I find all the monitoring to be much easier when I'm excited about the

result, though I wish I'd though ahead and starting drawing some form of constellation on my hand.

9:00am
Decided to eat Stouffer's Fish Filet meal and Snickers Protein bar before bed. Took 2 Prandin, but too lazy to check blood sugar.

5:38pm
Woke up shaking. Blood sugar at 57 mg/dl. Two Prandin apparently unnecessary when sleep is imminent. Drank a Boost and ate a Snicker's Protein Bar. Took 1 Prandin.

9:00pm
Pre-Meal: 83 mg/dl
I ate ¾ of Tombstone Pizza, half of a Diet Dr. Pepper and a watermelon Blow Pop. Was the Blow Pop necessary? No. Was it delicious? Yes. Though my sugar was a little low, I still took 2 Prandin because the pizza was loaded with carbs. I am lightly contemplating drinking some actual juice though. I'm like a junkie.

11:51pm
Pre-Meal: 158 mg/dl
I ate 3 hard shell Taco Bell tacos and 2 fresh apples with caramel dip. The dip had high fructose corn syrup, which I'm pretty sure is the greatest substance ever. I also

drank two cups of diet peach iced tea, which is most certainly not the greatest substance ever.

11/24/2008
2:31am
Post-Meal: 136 mg/dl
These numbers are not helping to keep me on diet soda.

7:30am
Fell asleep at some point. Woke up too lazy to check blood sugar, but with enough energy to make 4 fish filets (technically, Van De Kamp's made 'em...I just cooked 'em). I also ate a Slim Jim. One Prandin was involved.

3:00pm
Pre-Meal: 51 mg/dl
Once again awoke myself with low blood sugar. Had a Boost and ate a Snicker's Protein bar, this time without a Prandin. Apparently, I should not take those within two hours of bed time *(Note: I pulled that "two hour" thing straight out of my ass).*

8:00pm
Pre-Meal: 77 mg/dl
I ate a Big Mac, a medium fry, a medium vanilla shake and a medium orange drink/sprite (I mix the two). I took 3

Prandin. It's time to see what these things are made of.

10:48pm
Post-Meal: 163 mg/dl
Fuck you, diet soda. Fuck you straight to hell!
I decided to eat a Stouffer's Salisbury steak meal and two apples. I was hoping the apples would offset the massive amount of sodium in the meal (which also included macaroni and cheese).

11/25/2008
2:13am
Started to get the shakes. Ate two packets of sugar, Snickers Protein bar and a Blow Pop. Hand kinda hurt, so I didn't check blood sugar. Went to bed.

8:15am
Woke up and ate a large roast beef grinder. Didn't take a Prandin. Went back to bed.

2:30pm
Pre-Meal: 90 mg/dl
Stouffer's Fish Filet dinner and the last half of a Propel Fitwater (more like shitwater…) that I couldn't choke back last night. Just a stop gap meal before I hit some form of restaurant.

7:30pm
Went out, presumably to eat (at some point). Had a bit of an episode while in bookstore. Felt blood sugar dropping like thing that drops fast. Bought some root beer and drove home. Took blood sugar. Felt like I destroyed nerve in hand. By the time I got home my sugar was 96 mg/dl.

(No time stamp)
Ate large roast beef grinder, then immediately fell asleep. Running late for work. Blood sugar will have to wait.

11/26/2008
4:55am
Pre-Meal: 94 mg/dl
Two hot dogs, Swedish meatballs and three sausage links. Not my favorite meal, but I washed it down with ginger ale, made even more delicious by the fact that it is forbidden. It was a 2 Prandin operation.

7:40am
Post-Meal: 141 mg/dl
We can look at this one of two ways. I could either take fewer pills or eat more sugar. It looks like I'm going to be reunited with my one true love: high fructose corn syrup.

9:00pm
Pre-meal: 102 mg/dl

I think I've been pressing way too hard with the lancets. Perhaps this revelation will help prevent further nerve damage *(Note: I did not actually damage any nerves)*.

One bowl of chili, an A&W root beer and a Snicker's Protein bar. This is quite possibly the least diabetic friendly meal I've had *(Note: No, it's not)*.

11:20pm
Post-Meal: 190 mg/dl
Not exactly 2.5 hours after, but I had to leave for work.

11/27/2008
Checked at 1:00 am 'cause I was feelin' shaky. Verdict: 61 mg/dl
I had three sugar packets and 2 dark chocolate pearls. Not quite as creepy as it sounds. It's apparently some *(Note: I just stop writing here. Whatever those things were, they didn't help my concentration)*

4:47am
Pre-Meal: 87 mg/dl
I ate a pile of French fries coated with cheese and bacon bits, a cup of rice pilaf, a cup of corn chowder, two oatmeal raisin cookies and two cups of apple juice. 2 Prandin: No prisoners

7:34am
Post-Meal: 226 mg/dl

Whoops.

10:00pm
Pre-Meal: 97 mg/dl
I had three fish filets (fried) and a bowl of chili. Then decided to drink a root beer and eat a peanut butter and jelly sandwich. It was a Thanksgiving meal for the ages. I took 3 Prandin.

11/28/2008
12:30am
Post-Meal: 250 mg/dl
My return to regular soda may have been slightly premature. I took another Prandin.

4:13am
Pre-Meal: 93 mg/dl
I ate 3 slices of cherry zinfandel ham, 2 pieces of stuffed cod (I didn't eat the stuffing), some apple crisp-like substance (delicious) and day old carrot cake (not so delicious). I took 3 Prandin and washed it down with ginger ale. I'm not doing it to be reckless, just to see what these things do. It's science.

6:47am
Post-Meal: 118 mg/dl
What the fuck, Prandin? I'm going to start doing the math on exactly how much

sugar I eat, because I obviously can't wing it *(Note: I never start doing the math)*.

10:00pm
Pre-Meal: 98 mg/dl
I ate all but one slice of a Tombstone Pepperoni Pizza and some of the Cran-Apple diet drink. The pizza was very carb-y, so I took 3 Prandin.

11/29/2008
12:00am
Post-Meal: 143 mg/dl
I should have just drank a root beer.

3:14am
I took a Prandin so I could drink some apple juice. I was delicious.

4:19am
Pre-Meal: 181 mg/dl
I expected much worse.
3 chicken tacos, some bacon, a small amount of scallop and shrimp pasta (though I could find neither scallop nor shrimp in it), a small slice of carrot cake and a cup of ginger ale. I took 3 Prandin because I had already taken 1 an hour earlier.

7:00am
Post-Meal: 114 mg/dl
I swear I'll get this right someday.

9:30pm
I was very hungry and forgot to check my sugar before eating. Let's assume it was 98 mg/dl. I ate a large bowl of clam chowder, a small steak and an A&W Root Beer. I took 4 Prandin. Here's hoping for the best.

11/30/2008
Post-Meal: 149 mg/dl
Nailed it.

1:30am
Well, I thought I did. I didn't have time to check my sugars, but I got the shakes, so I had some hot chocolate and sugar-filled tea. All this makes my head hurt.

3:15am
Pre-Meal: 130 mg/dl
I had a double cheeseburger, cheddar and bacon fries, two slices of bacon and a slice of carrot cake. Washed it down with ginger ale and 2 prandins.

5:55am
Post-Meal: 125 mg/dl
Not bad.

12/3/2008
1:10am
Post-Meal: 201 mg/dl

Took some time off because the wheel almost fell off my car. Woke up late today. Ate Fritos Flavor Twists, 2 pieces of cold bacon pizza, Snicker's Protein bar and washed it down with Hawaiian Punch. I shouldn't have had the Hawaiian Punch, but I love the stuff that comes from the soda bottling plant.

4:45am
Pre-Meal: 64 mg/dl
Having started to feel the cold kiss of the no sugar shakes, I drank a Dr. Pepper, ate and oatmeal raisin cookie, had some pasta with sauce and meatballs, a few homefries with A1, half a fried cod filet (it was atrocious) and some way too crunchy bacon. I followed it with 2 root beers, a banana, another cookie and some carrot cake. I took 3 Prandin over the course of the meal.

7:30am
Post-Meal: 216 mg/dl
I over compensated for the low sugar. These things happen.

8:00pm
I can't find my meter right now, but my sugars feel pretty good and that's good enough for me. I'm having 6 potato perogies, flavor twists and a root beer. I'm taking 4 Prandins.

10:30pm
Post-Meal: 196 mg/dl
It's a little high, but it's going to drop like a stone. I know these things.

12/4/2008
1:30am
Got the shakes. Ate some candy. Had a Dr. Pepper. Couldn't stop eating candy. Delicious.

4:10am
Pre-Meal: 76 mg/dl
I had a bacon double cheeseburger, two slices of roast beef, French fries with A1, carrot cake and two cups of root beer. I took 2 Prandin due to the previous state of my sugars.

7:00am
Post-Meal: 77 mg/dl
I checked it twice just to make sure this was right. Worth noting that I took the Prandin slightly before meal time.

9:00pm
Pre-Meal: 88 mg/dl
Ate a pepperoni calzone and a Snicker's Energy bar. Washed it down with some Gatorade. Took Prandin (3) slightly ahead of time. Still kinda hungry, but didn't feel like making anything else.

11:15pm
Post-Meal: 136 mg/dl
Have to go to work, so had to check early. Seems a little low. Will call Dr. Pepper to even it out.

12/5/2008
4:13am
Pre-Meal: 116 mg/dl
I drank a Dr. Pepper so I didn't drop earlier (as in sugar levels, not actually droppin' on the floor). For lunch I had 2 sausage links, homefries with A1, one slice of bacon (it was horrible and 2 slice of carrot cake. Washed it down with Root Beer. Thinking about eating bag of Skittles I've had warming up in my pocket. Warmth unleashes their deliciousness.

6:50am
Post-Meal: 156 mg/dl
I think I may actually be getting good at this.

9:30pm
Pre-Meal: 106 mg/dl
In the morning, I did eat a PB+J sandwich, two clementine oranges and an A&W before I went to bed. Upon awakening, I enjoyed 3 slices of bacon pizza and 2 cups of Gatorade with 3 Prandin. For whatever reason, no one else in the house

has heard of bacon pizza. My grandmother thinks I invented it, though I know she's had it before.

12/6/2008
12:15am
Post-Meal: 150 mg/dl
I find that if I have a soda sometime after a meal, it keeps me from gettin' cranky.

4:10am
Pre-Meal: 51 mg/dl
Well, I thought the soda thing worked. I had 3 cups of apple juice, half a bag of skittles, a monte cristo, a pile of French fries, a couple of slices of bacon and a slice of carrot cake. I would have ate more, but I ran out of time. I took 3 Prandin.

7:10am
Post-Meal: 170 mg/dl
I got a little shaky yesterday morning, so I may follow up with some juice soon. Dr. Pepper would keep me up all day.

9:30pm
Forgot meter in car. Too cold for retrieval. Ate a pound of chicken and a cup of Gatorade. Took 2 Prandin.

12/7/2008
12:00am

Turns out that I only have one lancet left in pouch. Will save it for after lunch. Will continue to pretend I have plenty to get off these damn phones.

3:15am
I had 2 double cheeseburgers, French fries covered in meat lasagna (delicious!), a slice of carrot cake and a cup of apple juice. I have no idea what my sugar was before this, but I'll check the aftermath.

5:55am
Post-Meal: 89 mg/dl
I drank some apple juice right before this. Probably a good thing.

12/11/2008
1:30am
I had two cups of apple juice, a Snicker's Energy bar and two packets of sugar. I could feel my sugar dropping, so consider this a pre-emptive strike. Now that I'm doing decently with the Prandin, I got kinda lazy with the monitoring, though I've redoubled my efforts to break 140 lbs buck ass naked.

4:15am
I had rice pilaf, pulled pork, carrot cake and apple juice. I took two Prandin, but didn't check my blood sugar first because I'm lazy.

7:00am
Post-Meal: 180 mg/dl
Considering the amount of sugar that I've eaten today, I'm fairly impressed by this.

12/12/2008
Pre-Meal: 92 mg/dl
I had a large roast beef grinder, a root beer and a high protein Boost. I took 3 Prandin. Also, a Batman Fruit Roll-up.

1:16am
Phone started ringing, so I didn't get to check sugar. Kinda starting to feel low.

4:12am
Pre-Meal: 102 mg/dl
Double cheeseburger, French fries, bacon and carrot cake. I didn't have time to finish it all. One Dr. Pepper and one apple juice.

6:15am
Post-Meal: 152 mg/dl
A decent showing

8:30am
Ate a bowl of Frosted Flakes Gold
(note: this was a short lived variation on the Frosted Flakes formula that used a honey

glaze instead of frosting) and a Carnation Instant Breakfast. Went to bed.

    9:00pm
Ate at Denny's. Had Philly melt, seasoned fries and Pancake Puppies, which are tiny round pancakes covered in sugar and cinnamon. Trying really hard to not throw up. Meal was, however, delicious first time around. Washed down with Cherry Coke.

    This is apparently the point where I decided that I'm great at diabetes, because the diary just stops here. As I mentioned in the introduction, I continued to make adjustments to both my diet and pill intake, but I didn't keep a diary of all that, so you'll just have to take my word for it.

######

Acknowledgements

The process of writing this book was much harder than I thought it would be. Here's a list of people who made it easier on me.

Thanks to my family for putting up with me. Particularly Dad and Linda for ensuring that this book didn't end with me homeless and Mom and Paul for always helping me out when I need it (which is a lot). Also, thanks to Jake for unknowingly serving as the control in my thought experiment.

The staff at Yale New Haven Hospital has kept me alive for 30 years, so I suppose they deserve some of the blame for what you just read. The AQI group also served as unwitting test audiences for some of the pieces in this book. Thank you Robyn Scatena MD (who pointed me towards the title for the book), Cheryl Robacynski RD, Jonathan Koff MD, Sue Iezzi RN, Jennifer Sullivan-Kelley LCSW, Clemente Britto MD, Marjorie Ardito RT, Margaret Nemetz PT, Kristy Merrit RT, and Jaideep Talwalkar MD.

The Forbes family is like a second family to me. They've never made me feel like the intruder I often am. Particular thanks goes to Gams, Walter, Andy (who took both the front cover and author photos), Tom (who came up with the concept for the cover photo), Ed, Cathy, Helen and however many kids are now running around with the Forbes name.

I think it's kind of stupid to thank someone who's dead, because it's not like they're going to read the book, but this would feel empty if I didn't mention Grandpa Bill. I should thank Grama Marion as well, though she's still alive. If she'd let me get her a damn hearing aid, I'd read the book to her. As it stands, I might just try playing her the audio version.

Thank you to Bentley McBentleson for not letting me forget that I promised him a book 8 years ago.

In the course of my work day, I ended up trying out revisions by talking to a number of people who had no idea I was using them as a focus group. I don't want to name any names—mostly because I'm scared I'd leave someone out—but if they read the book and recognize a story, I'm sure they'll figure it out. Thank you for not telling me to shut up.

Thanks to Scottmichael Farrey for letting me eat all the jalapeno coins.

Bonnie. *nods* Darcy. *nods*

And finally I must thank the one who could not escape these stories, the one for whom they exist, my Bekka. She helped me shape this thing— acting as both editor and cheerleader— and gave it purpose. I'm glad to be part of her life and I thank her and her family for taking a chance on some dude from the internet. I love you, Babe!

Oh yeah, and thank you for reading. I hope it wasn't as painful to read as it was to write.

About the Author

Jay Gironimi makes music at allhallowsevil.org and words at canteatcantbreathe.com. His last name rhymes with astronomy.

Twitter: http://twitter.com/allhallowsevil